PUZZLEQUIZ

PUZZLEQUIZ

Wit Twisters, Brain Teasers, Riddles, Puzzles, and Tough Questions

By Stephen Barr

illustrated by Colos

PERENNIAL LIBRARY

Harper & Row, Publishers, New York
Grand Rapids, Philadelphia, St. Louis, San Francisco
London, Singapore, Sydney, Tokyo, Toronto

LIBRARY OF CONGRESS CATALOG CARD NUMBER 89-46070

ISBN 0-06-091974-4

90 91 92 93 94 FG 10 9 8 7 6 5 4 3 2 1

Don't Take Anything For Granted

Consider the atoms;
They toil not, but they spin like crazy
Until everything gets hazy.
The electrons are worse;
They have an intense desire to disperse.
No one should ridicule this propensity
Because it reduces their density.
As for alpha and beta particles
And such articles
Too small to seem to matter at all,
Watch it—the Decline and Fall
Was due to ignoring the small-but-busy.
The emperors went around saying, Who is he?
And the first consuls would say to ignore 'em,
They don't even amount to a quorum,
In fact we don't want 'em.
Then along came the quantum,
To say nothing of the Goth,
And we all know about the Candle and the Moth;
Only this time the Moth blew out the Candle,
But he was unable to handle
Things any better than the emperor could,
So knock on wood.

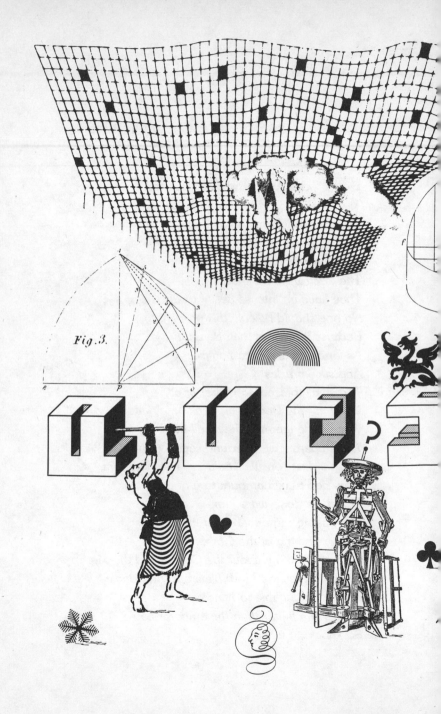

Fig. 3.

QUESTIONS

The answers to the puzzles follow question number 538.

1 A man falls from the twentieth floor of a building and lands unhurt: What very common thing saves him?

2 What was the first transplant?

3 What do we sit on that has only two legs, and a back that we don't lean against?

4 What is it that flies, but has no wings, propeller or gas bag?

5 What has eight wheels but carries only one passenger?

6 "Monday six letters hath." Which day of the week has none?

7 If its final *e* is deleted, this six-letter word becomes the plural form of the kind of statement it usually begins. (Both are common English words.)

8 What is the most expensive foodstuff sold in supermarkets? How much is it per pound?

9 Arrange the nine digits in a 3-by-3 square so that they add up the same vertically, horizontally and through both diagonals, in each case working through the middle digit.

10 What was the first plastic, still in wide use?

11 In World War I the Germans were allowed to "dis-

cover" a map showing the location of mines in the sea—most of which did not exist. How exactly did this help the English?

12 In this picture there are some places for words: speech balloons and signs. Fill them in à la TV and Madison Avenue.

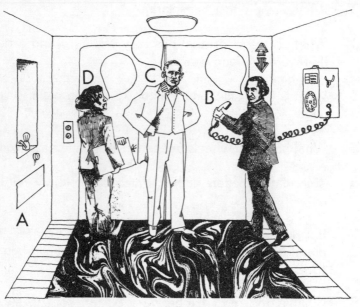

13 In what country is the oldest all-wood building that has been in continuous use for the same purpose throughout its history?

14 And what is the oldest manufactory still operating on its original site?

15 Where and when was the first automobile driven?

16 In Caesar's famous remark about the division of Gaul

into three parts, what was the actual order of his words? The answer can be in English.

17 What were the first words on (a) *the telegraph,* (b) *the telephone,* (c) *the phonograph?*

18 Who invented the first workable electric light and when?

19 Which of these pairs of words are mutually cognate (i.e., from or containing the same root)?
(a) *miniature, miniscule;* (b) *thunder, tendon;* (c) *hide, cuticle;* (d) *hen, chanticleer;* (e) *apricot, precocious;* (f) *water, inundate.*

20 We are on the International date line facing north. It's Monday on the left and Tuesday to the right. Where else on earth do these two days meet?

21 People frequently fail oral tests because they don't listen to the questions carefully; if you pay strict attention, these practically answer themselves:

(a) *Offhand can you think of a nine-letter English word ending in* u?
(b) *And the next one is a word with* ghb *in it?*
(c) *You say you don't know an anagram of* coasting?
(d) *What is the same as a plateau?*
(e) *Only the wise, in conjunction, know a three-syllable word with no* a, e, i, o *or* u *in it!*
(f) *So you claim you don't believe there's a one-syllable word with four different vowels in a row together?*
(g) *Well, what is a one-word anagram of* new door?

22 In the quotation, "Hoist with his own petard," what sort of a point did the petard have?

23 Why is it an advantage to have a constantly running electric fan in a room heated by a wood or kerosene stove, but not in one heated by a big fireplace?

24 What do *pleasance* and *haha* have in common?

25 When Little Jack Horner put in his thumb and pulled out a plum, what was referred to?

26 What was the *wayzgoose*?

27 What are the three primary colors?

28 What was the name and date of the most violent of known volcanic eruptions?

29 Define (a) *odontology*, (b) *puisne*, (c) *zymology*, (d) *cordwainer*, (e) *jean*, (f) *burke*.

30 What was the first use made of the scientific theory that Archimedes is said to have discovered in his bath, crying "Eureka!"?

31 Fill in the beginnings of these one-syllable common English words, all of which have the same rhyme: —ARD, —ERD, —IRD, —ORD, —URD.

32 Draw a lion's face based on ten equal circles, and a horse based on three unequal ovals.

33 What do these lines of letters mean or signify?
ETAOINSHRDLU, etc.
SCPATMEDRFIN, etc.

34 "Prove" that 1 = 0. Hint: try using factorials.

35 *The Mirror.* We all know that a mirror reverses you (apparently) from left-to-right, but not head-to-foot. But do you know why?

36 What do the following have in common?
Francis Bellamy, Kenyon Cox, Elbert Hubbard, Abbot Lawrence Lowe, Robert Peary, Henri Pétain, G. Bernard Shaw, Booker T. Washington, Kate Douglas Wiggin, Oscar Wilde, Woodrow Wilson and Sigmund Freud.

37 If, in a vacuum, you hang two objects of the same weight by two strings of the same length they will swing in time with one another. If you increase the length of one string its weight will swing slower. What will happen if you increase one weight?

38 *Small Crossword.*

ACROSS: 1. Sacred tree. 3. Weisman's unit of germ plasm.
DOWN: 1. Symbol of gray metal. 2. Base of mesmerism.

39 What single word describes a kind of fly, boot, andiron, soldier and coarse sacking?

40 How does the present population of the little town of Bethlehem in Israel compare with that of Nantucket Island?

41 This mini-crossword has four different words in it, all of which have the same definition. Fill it in.

42 Apropos of Hamlet saying that he knew a hawk from a handsaw, many people have said that all you need to do is leave them both out in the rain, and see which rusts. What's wrong?

43 What is wrong with the date 6/91/9?

44 Where does the following phrase first occur?
Of the People, by the People and for the People.

45 We have two hands, apes have four. What has three?

46 What do the following have in common?
Chain, railway, running, loop.

47 The cook spilled some X on a piece of paper and, being next to the stove, it dried quickly after having soaked through the sheet. Then the paper blew out of the window and down the hill and into a cave. Here it was discovered 1,000 years later perfectly preserved by X. What was X? (Common in kitchens.)

48 A and B both claim to be, solely, guilty of murdering X. How can the judge make sure the guilty one suffers the ordained penalty without punishing the innocent one?

49 These two four-letter words are partly covered. All three have the same two consonants at the end and all three o's are pronounced differently; what are they?

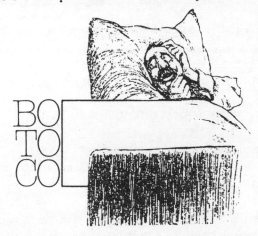

50 There is a small kitchen with a big refrigerator in it

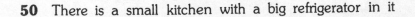

whose storage volume is a hundredth of the kitchen's; it is summer. To what extent would the refrigerator cool the kitchen if it were left open and running with the kitchen at 100 degrees?

51 When was the slide fastener first invented and in common use?

52 What kind of literary work does an author presumably never finish?

53 What is the most difficult movement to make with the fingers that doesn't involve strength or contortion?

54 When can you correctly say *different than?*

55 What movement made by which muscle or limb or limbs is, without using any object such as a lever, the most powerful the human body is capable of?

56 Which is the faster, blinking the eyes shut or opening them?

57 What is the easiest length for an anagram?

58 Which letter is most often silent in English?

59 What does this sentence suggest to you?
Won tooth-reef, or, if Ives Ickes even ate an eye-antenna.

60 A man is heating liquid A which will be mixed with liquid B, now cold. If he continues heating A, the resultant mixture of A and B will be less hot than if he were to mix it now. Why?

61 Using a succession of equal squares, design a full alphabet with the addition of small intrusions at the edges, i.e., cut-off corners, various-shaped dots inside, etc.

62 If you knew that a roulette wheel is honestly run, and red has come up nineteen times, what should you bet on the twentieth?

63 What's odd about the animal on the Camel cigarette packages?

64 The centaur had four legs and two arms. Of what is that true today?

65 Policeman A will refrain from arresting you for fifty dollars, but policeman B will for a mere five bucks. Which is the more venal?

66 Where in the world can one look north and south, but not east or west? (At the north pole one can't look north.)

67 The artist Esher is famous for his "ambiguous" illustrations; an example, not by him, is shown here. Can you do one in two short lines?

68 Two quarters are flat on a table and touching. If we are only allowed to touch one quarter without moving it and move the other without touching it, how can we put a dime between them? The table may not be moved and we may not blow.

69 What are 37 degrees centigrade and 29.5 degrees Reaumur?

70 A modern country house has a gable equilateral-triangular in shape in which the owner wants to cut a square window as big as possible (see figure). Ignoring frames, etc., what is the size of the window compared to the gable?

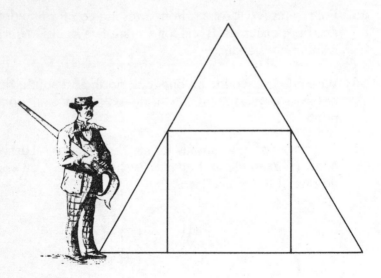

71 Of what kind of glass were medieval mirrors made?

72 The figure shows a typical Gothic arch; what is *h* equal to? To be solved in the head without drawing anything, in two minutes.

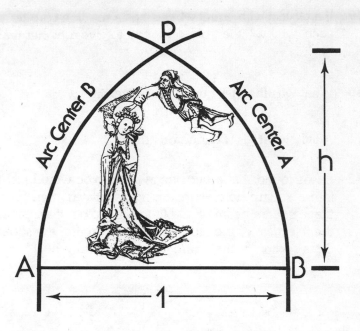

73 Why is a certain useful metal called *nickel?*

74 Who said "Let them eat cake"?

75 Prior to World War II what was the only country that ever declared war on the United States?

76 For what should Matthew Henson be remembered?

77 What, according to the Bible, "goeth before a fall"?

78 How old was Methuselah actually when he died?

79 If a bicycle with equal wheels has a rotation counter on each, why will the front one tend to give a higher reading?

80 What was the first European university?

81 A little what "is a dangerous thing"?

82 It was found that a very thin-walled pipe would just fit into a square hole as in the figure. It was then found that a square beam would fit into the pipe. If we ignore the thickness of the pipe, what is the area of the square cross section of the beam compared to the hole?

83 Name who wrote the following: the song "Sally in Our Alley"; the (I believe) longest two invented words in the English language; and the song "God Save the King."

84 Why was the old (Asia Minor) duodecimal system better than our decimal one?

85 How far west of Reno, which is 200 miles inland from the Pacific, is Los Angeles?

86 What is the southernmost part of the continental United States?

87 *For Topologists.* Draw or cut out of paper a flat surface that has one side and three edges all interlocked but none linked.

88 The meaning of a word can change with the passage of years. What were the old meanings of the following words?
villain, knave, uncouth, right, wrong, spirit, girl, infant.

89 A man poured exactly one pint of sugar into a cylindrical glass pint jar. Owing to his pouring it through a small hole, it humped up in the middle, finally making an exact cone the base of which was just an inch below the rim of the jar. How far above the rim was the apex of the cone? (This can be done in the head if certain formulas are remembered.)

90 What were the real names of Voltaire, Joseph Conrad and Anatole France?

91 "If I were to offer you some _____, I think you'd _____ it." What single word fills both blanks?

92 Why is it that when we are on a moving train and we see vertically falling rain the paths of the drops appear slanted, whereas the telegraph poles at the side of the track, although they are exactly parallel to the locus of any given drop, appear vertical?

93 What were the four neighboring colonies that first called themselves New England?

94 What was the first English newspaper and when did it appear?

95 What (to our present knowledge) was the first newspaper anywhere?

96 What are the largest living things?

97 What are the largest animals that ever lived?

98 What keeps the dome of Saint Paul's in London from bursting its seams?

99 What is the most important difference between the Roman and Arabic number systems?

100 What tipped off the anthropologists to the fact that the cave paintings in Australia were not very ancient?

101 What two-syllable English word meaning "something sharp" can be changed by adding *ss* at the end to "something not wanted"?

102 What is unusual about the name of the orchestral instrument the basset horn?

103 What is a tinker's dam?

104 A well-known tongue-twister begins Peter Piper, etc.; what is a far harder and simpler one?

105 More or less where, without exact calculation, is the shortest bisector of the area of an equilateral triangle?

106 What three things is Benjamin Franklin credited with inventing?

107 What is the biggest finite number that can be expressed with four 4's, using any mathematical operational symbols like !(factorial) or brackets, etc.? Remember, however, that (n!)!)!) is inadmissible.

108 What timepiece has the fewest number of moving parts?

109 What timepiece has the greatest number of moving parts?

110 What was our first electrical gadget?

111 In what respects is "Sumer is Icumen in" remarkable?

112 For what purpose was brandy originally made?

113 What was the first chemical additive to food in wide use?

114 What does the *bel* in *belfry* mean?

115 What is the biggest Roman number that spells an English word?

116 What famous philanthropist lived to be over one hundred years old?

117 How can a smallish room be cooled in hot weather without any air conditioning?

118 Where was dry cleaning started as a regular business?

119 Why are many younger people under the impression that the old silent films were too fast and jerky?

120 What is the largest single sheet of paper normally seen by the average American during an ordinary day?

121 What was the origin of the red-and-white-striped barber pole?

122 In what way is Melba toast named after two people?

123 If you are indoors, what should you do if a tornado is approaching?

124 Which of our "five" senses is least understood and why?

125 What are or were the following made of?
(a) *the hard base of billiard table tops,* (b) *old victrola records,* (c) *Ping-Pong balls,* (d) *ocean fishing net floats,* (e) *the striking surface of safety match books and boxes,* (f) *the lead-in wire where it goes through the glass of early electric light bulbs,* (g) *nylon,* (h) *the first window panes.*

126 To be done in the head. Give the dimensions of the arrangement of the fifty-two 2″-by-3″ cards of a deck laid flat that most nearly approximates a solid square.

127 Are bacteria animal or vegetable?

128 Of what language is *ayah?*

129 Identify what the following is an example of: HIUNDRATATATARIRE.

130 Divide the rectilinear right-angled figure shown into two equal areas with one straight line through P. Prove.

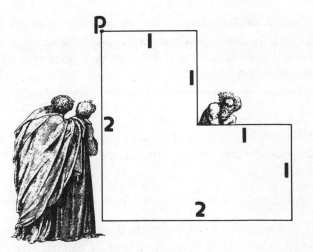

131 What widely popular dish of food was brought back from the east by Marco Polo?

132 To be done in the head, but with a chess board in front of you. State which chess piece, starting from its own square, can make a complete tour of the board in the least number of moves. *A tour here means passing through all squares. A knight is regarded as jumping and so takes 63 moves.*

133 In your head, work out the approximate volume, in terms of liquid capacity, of a human body that weighs about 160 pounds.

134 When ancient Byzantium was enlarged and refounded by the early Christians, to what was its name first changed?

135 Cyrano de Bergerac is widely remembered as being the inspiration of Edmond Rostand's famous play; what other literature did he inspire that is also well known?

136 The presence of sand on sandpaper enables it to fulfill its function, as does the news on newspaper and carbon on carbon paper; but X paper is not helped by X on it. What is X?

137 If a newspaper had been published in London in 1492, what would have been the biggest headline story?

138 Of what was Cinderella's slipper made?

139 C is the center of a circle. What are A, B and D called?

140 What is the biggest country on the equator?

141 Give a four-letter word that rhymes with neither *eely* nor *elly* and yet ends with *ely*.

142 With what phrase does *Beowulf* begin?

143 Bartlett credits the colloquialism "Gives the nod" to Homer; how is this misleading?

144 When and by whom was optical projection of moving objects first done? Also, when did the talkies start?

145 The Pilgrims came over in the Mayflower, Columbus in the Santa Maria, Niña and Pinta. What ships did Captain John Smith and the first Jamestown settlers come in?

146 What are Thailand and Siberia called by the people who live there?

147 Prior to the Empire State (built in 1929) what, in chronological order, were the three tallest buildings in New York?

148 What famous singer is remembered for having kept his audience from hearing other singers?

149 What is the mistake usually made about the difference of U.S. from English pronunciation of *either?*

150 What were the first automatic safety devices in elevators?

151 Who was the most famous philosopher to die at about thirty years of age?

152 Which numbers marked on the hour positions of a clock can be indicated by more than two numerals?

153 Where did the first European occupants of Iceland come from?

154 What's the farthest north in Europe that palm trees grow out of doors?

155 If a letter comes through the mail and the stamp hasn't been cancelled, how do you tear it off the envelope?

156 Where and how is the (Greek) letter π (Pi) given the value of three in the Bible?

157 How useful are the theories of the Facial Angle and the Cephalic Index?

158 What famous name for the U.S. flag is connected with the mutiny on the Bounty?

159 Give a five-letter word that's all vowels (no y's).

160 Which is the fastest of birds?

161 For what reason in the original Linotype did they decide not to put both *q* and *u* on the same piece of type?

162 State what's wrong with the name *mineral oil*.

163 Frequently in movies someone falls from a high place and we hear his loud continuous cry of horror growing less loud as he recedes from us downward. What is the common error in this sound effect?

164 We start with a paper rhombus (see figure).
Show a method of repeatedly folding with a similar fold each time but not a series of parallel folds, so that an indefinite number of smaller and smaller triangles are produced *ad infinitum*.

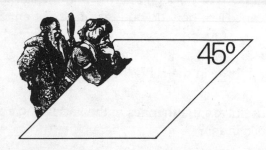

165 What well-known French word spelled backwards gives its translation, a word which describes something of which the United States is made up?

166 What smells perfectly dreadful that is used to make something that smells perfectly lovely?

167 What famous opera composer had no librettist?

168 What does the Piltdown skull tell us about humanity?

169 Describe the "French" kitchen knife and explain its value in cutting and slicing piled-up slices.

170 What does one golf-watching flea say to another?

171 Describe what you should do when you try hard but can't quite unscrew the top of a new jar.

172 What is the longest piece of metal in the world?

173 What nine-letter English word meaning "scoundrel" can be successively cut at the beginning to give altogether four words of different origins totally unconnected in meaning?

174 What animal climbs itself?

175 What exactly is a *forlorn hope?*

176 Eggs with few exceptions are slightly narrower at one end. What useful purpose does this serve?

177 What is immediately recognized by all Americans and Europeans but for which there is *no* name?

178 Explain the words *Roundhead* and *Cavalier.*

179 What fire was the most damaging to literature in all history?

180 What artist made a kind of chinaware famous although it was not named after him, but somebody else?

181 Switzerland is usually thought of as the oldest existing democracy. What is a rival claimant?

182 It is a felony to make a photograph of American currency even if there is no intention of passing it, yet it is allowed on television. Why?

183 About how much later than the Authorized Version—the King James Bible—was the Douay Bible finished?

184 What plural English word is made singular by putting *y* in front?

185 Give the circumstances under which a medical doctor is no longer to be treated as one.

186 What does this statement suggest? "J. F. Mam? J. J. as on D!"

187 What is even more imprecise and common than calling a spider a bug?

188 What kind of foreign word is used in the following? "That's a lot of bosh."

189 Give a simple and relatively legal way to avoid paying income tax (you won't get away with it).

190 In which state is East Chicago?

191 What have the Russian Ballet and Wagnerism in common?

192 What is the longest-lived thing?

193 When something makes a loud bang between us and the side of a house or a cliff, we hear it and its echo. What would we hear if the source of sound were touching the surface?

194 How does the tensile strength of nylon compare with that of steel?

195 What is the fundamental difference between white rice and wild rice?

196 In what profession is one not supposed to do what the profession's name implies?

197 Where and approximately when did the modern classical ballet originate?

198 People frequently say *solipsism* when they mean *solecism*. Explain their mistake.

199 A and B had scallops for dinner, served in a dish from which they both helped themselves. At the end they left six in the dish. "I ate more than you did," said A. "No," said B, "we each left three in the dish." Explain why B's reasoning was wrong.

200 How do spiders make a round web? In what order are its parts laid out? (Experiment with pencil and paper.)

201 What are the six "Simple Machines" as usually given?

202 From how far away can thunder be heard?

203 From how many directions can the local weather be affected?

204 Describe and make a piece of paper that will tear into more than two pieces when pulled at its ends.

205 Braille is the name of the alphabet that enables the blind to "see" and read with their fingers. What is the name of the alphabet that enables the deaf to "hear"?

206 How can two commonly used writing implements give you an indication of the weather?

207 Where, when and by whom was the Encyclopedia Britannica first produced, and who was its editor?

208 Give a singular—with no *s* in it—English word with five consonants occurring in succession.

209 Name and describe the four basic kinds of bridges.

210 Give some examples of common expletives; no "four-letter words."

211 What kind of woodworking is done in most offices?

212 What was Rome originally?

213 What does mead taste like?

214 When opposing counsel, backed by judge, tells you to "answer yes or no," how can you get around it?

215 A piece of paper is found that is known to be the directions for getting a fortune in diamonds. It says on it, "3 left, 12 right, 16 left, 8 right." Explain what it means.

216 What is the all-time best-seller book?

217 What can the relative length of two bars made of a non-expanding alloy indicate? (We assume atoms are indefinitely small.)

218 What style of painting, when done realistically, uses the three true primary colors, red, green and violet?

219 What, from statistical records, is the most dangerous job in America?

220 How many tastes can the tongue perceive?

221 What word has *iea* in it, you sleepy person?

222 Editors often insist on your writing "It is I," not "me." How can one show them they're full of hot air?

223 Some people think that Washington D.C. deserves a star on the flag like a state. How can 51 stars make a reasonable pattern?

224 If someone says "I feel badly," what does the statement mean?

225 What is peculiar about the naming of wind directions?

226 What characterizes the following statement?
A boastful Canadian dog emitted frightening growls, his ivory jaws knifing like mad. "No one pants quite right!" said the Labrador, "unless voiced with xylophones, you zebras!"

227 How can you cut out a piece of paper, bounded by straight lines all either parallel or at right angles, that can be bent to cover three adjacent sides of a five-inch cube? The arbitrary rule is that at no point is the paper to be more than one inch wide, though it eventually gets laterally joined.

228 In four lines describe what to do to make your cat happy.

229 Which of the continental United States is (excluding islands) completely divided into non-touching large parts?

230 Where did Edgar A. Poe first go to school? And did he write any novels?

231 Give the origin and original meaning of *Hey Rube!*

232 Most metals cost far more in the United States than they did at the beginning of the century; what metal is on the contrary far cheaper now than then?

233 *For Higher Math bugs.* Fill out and explain this equation: $\infty xi = ?$

234 In terms of U.S. landmarks, how far south does Canada reach?

235 Identify this orchestral piece of music. (To be played in any key.)

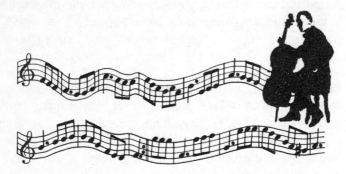

236 What well-known English word has *ii* in it?

237 Give the shape of a paper helix which when supported by one end could hang with equally spaced turns to an indefinite distance.

238 Approximately how much would a man 44,000 miles tall weigh if he were in Sumatra?

239 The correct answer to the following question should not be too hard to arrive at. We all know that *news* has the four points of the compass in it—*n*orth, *e*ast, *w*est and *s*outh. So does *wens*. Can you think of a very common six-letter word with the same four letters clumped in the middle?

240 What is this?
SAVIGIKSINIARIARTOKASUAROMARYOTIT-
TOGOG.

241 What accident to whose hand gave great music to the world?

242 Considering that most people are right-handed, what is rather odd about typewriters?

243 Approximately how many cells are in an egg yolk?

244 What did Alexander Hamilton and Aaron Burr fight their duel about?

245 The longest section in Bartlett's *Familiar Quotations* is Shakespeare. What is the shortest?

246 What did Admiral Farragut actually say with regard to the torpedoes and going forward in spite of them?

247 The tones of most musical instruments are varied by altering the length of what vibrates. With what well-known wind instrument are changes in pitch made by stopping holes with the fingers without length coming into it? Give its name and describe a natural sound phenomenon to which it is akin.

248 There is said to be a nearly worldwide sign language dating back many centuries and still surviving in many places. Unlike the mutually differing speech languages it is universally almost the same. It is not confined to primitive tribes; can you give the most common examples that we all use?

249 Who, according to the ancient Greeks, was the first woman?

250 Who, after Saint Peter, was the first pope?

251 What was the first recorded name of the city of Paris?

252 What big building was originally on the site of the Cathedral of Notre Dame de Paris?

253 What is the disadvantage of a spiral staircase?

254 What is odd about the pronunciation of *aged?*

255 To what extent is fire implied by the word *immolation?*

256 If you wanted a mural painted in your living room and were given the choice of Hitler or Mozart, which would you choose?

257 What was the chief occupation of the poet Omar Khayyám?

258 Name the largest lake in Europe.

259 In what country and when was opium first declared illegal?

260 Describe how an icicle can form that is definitely longer than its tensile strength can support.

261 A man has a nonrectangular swimming pool. He takes out a large spotlight to illuminate it at night and by a weird accident the rays of the lamp light up the entire water surface but none of the surroundings. Give the probable shape of the pool and explain.

262 Where and what or who is *Ushant?*

263 How far west did the United States extend by the end of the eighteenth century?

264 What excellent, highly regarded English mathematician became world famous for a totally different expertise?

265 If a very strong, very tall man and a normally strong, rather short man want to reach as high as possible, who should stand on whose shoulders?

266 The Suez Canal connects the Mediterranean to the Red Sea. At what date did a connection first exist?

267 What's the heaviest piece of three-legged furniture?

268 What was the nationality of the inventor of the first telephone?

269 A well-known rebus is

STAND	TAKE	TO	TAKING
I	YOU	THROW	MY

translated as I understand you undertake to overthrow my undertaking. Give what might be called a rebus^2.

270 Time limit ten seconds: which is the least frequent digit used in the list of integers from 0 to 99?

271 What causes the bends in deep-sea diving?

272 What orchestral devices are not blown, bowed, plucked or struck?

273 What writing instrument is only used to write on its own material?

274 How are maps copyrighted?

275 Is the marine sponge animal, vegetable or mineral?

276 *Scope* as part of a word means see or view. In what instance does it definitely mean neither?

277 The ancient "scientists" said the four elements were Earth, Air, Fire and Water. What did the medieval doctors call the four "Humours"?

278 What is the northernmost point of the United States?

279 To a complete stranger, what was the most notable thing about George Washington?

280 Give an English word that has all six vowels in their alphabetical order, and no other vowels.

281 With one each of the nine digits, excluding zero, and any mathematical symbols, make a statement equal to one.

282 Which ship was undoubtedly the biggest prior to 1700?

283 What is the most unique thing about the Leaning Tower of Pisa?

284 What is the highest construction in New York City that is not made even partly of steel?

285 In what respect does the Veldt differ from steppes, pampas and the prairies?

286 Give the approximate distance between the Isles of Langerhans and the Semicircular Canals.

287 State what the following suggests, musically.
Cold cuts don't brown, can dry; each end fits each, don't cry; dough can be cooked.

288 What is the riddle connected with the Sphinx?

289 About how tall was the Great Pyramid compared to the Eiffel Tower?

290 On what grounds was Sir Walter Raleigh condemned to death?

291 For what was ramie highly regarded sixty years ago?

292 In the early part of this century, painting on the back of glass enjoyed a passing artistic vogue. How did one start such a work?

293 What kind of electric ray never goes faster than 10,000 mph?

294 Describe the black pepper plant.

295 Top hats are cylinders, bowlers are hemispheres and fool's caps, cones; what headgear used to be a fourth geometrical shape?

296 What was the title, date and name of the composer of the first opera?

297 When were the first postage stamps issued and where?

298 *To be done in the head.* A man cuts a wedge as shown from a cylindrical section of flat-ended sausage weighing ten pounds. What did the section weigh?

299 Hydrogen is so called because it generates water (Greek *hydro*); for what is oxygen named?

300 The series 0, 2, 6, 12, 20, 30, etc., is produced by successively adding the even numbers to the previous sums: 0, $0+2=2$, $2+4=6$, $6+6=12$, $12+8=20$, etc. What completely different method gives the same?

301 When Nero fiddled as Rome burned, who did he blame for the fire?

302 The precursor of James Watt's steam engine was Thomas Savery's. For what was the latter's steam engine used?

303 An ingenious thief, hoping to put the police off, left an earring, a glass with lipstick on it and some faked fingerprints. How did he do the latter?

304 You are on top of a dry, brush-covered mesa from which you can only climb down at the south end. A fire starts at that end which you have no means of extinguishing. There is a strong north wind. With no one to help you, what should you do to escape the fire?

305 Where are almost exactly circular lakes to be found?

306 What was the primary cause of Hans Christian Andersen's death?

307 Which major American city has no serially numbered streets?

308 Who was the first astronomer to maintain that the earth revolves around the sun?

309 To what do the words *basinet* and *sallet* both refer?

310 Name two ladies with the first name George who became famous.

311 Who was the most world-renowned person to play Hamlet in the nineteenth century?

312 What is the longest continuous mountain range in the world?

313 What is unique about the river Nile?

314 How did William the Conqueror feel about capital punishment and how many suffered it during his reign?

315 "I am not even seven," wailed Stanley, throwing tricycles . . . What kind of word should come next?

316 Give the distinction between a *catastrophe* and a *cataclysm*.

317 From the intestines of what animals are violin strings made?

318 What is most unusual about the following sentence?
As a doctor of psychiatry I can only say what I think is apropos of this killing: I don't know who did it, in fact I don't want to know, but I am afraid that any man or woman who would do such a thing is obviously mad, and should go to an institution for lunatics and similar unlucky humans.

319 What are the heaviest of all insects?

320 If you feel you absolutely must make a drawing, and have no pencil, crayon, pen or brush, but merely paper, white watercolor paint, a roller to put it on with and one place setting of the family silver, how do you go about it?

321 Besides being a famous voyager and naval man, for what other activity is Captain James Cook remembered?

322 Give the perspective view of an object that looks like (a) from above, (b) from the side, (c) from the front.

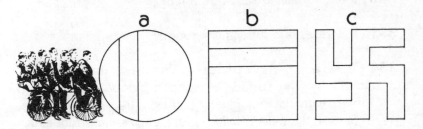

323 How much is a *Lakh?* And why is the name inappropriate?

324 What is hoarfrost?

325 About how much did the Cullinan Diamond weigh before cutting?

326 What was the first prototype of the piano?

327 Further back we explained how to make a silverpoint "etching." What else can we do to make an etching without a metal plate or acid?

328 "Passed away" and "Flew from false fear in finest flowerhood" both can be used to describe dying. What two rather similar words define the two types of wording?

329 What time of year was called the *Sprout-kale* by the Anglo-Saxons?

330 For what art was Leonardo Vinci known?

331 What do Parisians call cops (slang excluded)?

332 How did Galileo start out in life?

333 How does one fumigate a room?

334 Circles and parts of circles of different diameters can be made on the surface of spheres (globes) by cutting them with flat, imaginary planes. The ones with the greatest diameter, called great circles, are made by planes that pass through the center of the sphere. What border in the United States, excluding Alaska, follows a great circle of the earth for the longest distance?

335 What is so unusual about Gruyère cheese?

336 In what play does Mrs. Grundy appear?

337 Estimate the length of the relatively small-looking island Madagascar, located next to Africa.

338 When the British government many years ago decided to map the entire country by fitting aerial shots together, it ended up by costing them nothing. Why?

339 Without changing the order of the letters give a one-word anagram of two words: the first is something rather dreadful, the second by no means so.

340 What is the difference between a *shambles* and a *holocaust?*

341 Which Europeans first inhabited Iceland?

342 What English town's name is a translation of *Bosporus?*

343 *For Origamians.* Using only six folds, mark a square of paper so as to produce a square 1/5 of the original in area.

344 How should one feel after eating two large heads of lettuce?

345 When did the sulfur Lucifer match first come into use?

346 Define the derivative meanings of *voyage* and *journey.*

347 Who was Adam's first wife?

348 State what is wrong with the following sentence.
A pleonasm is redundant and tautological.

349 How much brighter approximately is the midday sun than the full moon?

350 Under whose rule was Pennsylvania from 1633 to 1654?

351 What French nineteenth-century artist used as a

pseudonym the French spelling of the Russian word for a type of drawing instrument?

352 Name four famous women astronomers.

353 What does *checkmate* mean literally?

354 What foolish and unnecessary act on the part of the British army triggered the Indian Mutiny in 1857?

355 Where did the posse of the Old West originate?

356 With an unlimited number of dimes, arrange three as illustrated in a straight line, using no ruler or other instruments.

357 Describe the first (English) railways.

358 In the Middle Ages scientists thought there were five elements. Four of them were Earth, Air, Fire and Water. What was the fifth?

359 What is ironic about prussic acid?

360 Who was the first governor of Rhode Island (1663)?

361 What is the first recorded and most famous "Irish bull" (i.e., a blunder in speech—once thought to be typical of the Irish)?

362 Express 100 by using all nine digits (excluding zero) three times each.

363 What did Napoleon say his soldiers all carried?

364 Who was the first woman to hold the semi-official position of recognized mistress of the French king?

365 Who invented spectacles (optical)?

366 Who was the first woman to hold the degree of Doctor of Medicine?

367 Of what word is *sovereignty* a modification?

368 What disaster occurred when Lord Dundreary appeared on the American stage?

369 What flying bird is the tallest, when standing?

370 Which world-famous actress first became well known for playing transvestite parts?

371 In criminal parlance, who do the following stand for? *Dip, hooker, cannon.*

372 What did Gilbert Stuart, J. M. Whistler and John Sargent have in common?

373 What was the most famous address in Baker Street, London?

374 Give the most famous and elaborate spoonerism on record. (A spoonerism is a transposition of initial sounds, such as saying "It's a dine fay" for "It's a fine day.")

375 What led to the name Jehovah?

376 Who lived the longest of the great European artists?

377 Which is the nearest star, and about how far away is it?

378 What was the expertise of Swedenborg before he became a mystic?

379 Comment on this picture of a snake walking.

380 Why were Morris dancers so called?

381 When did Portugal become a separate country?

382 What was the first Italian opera produced in Paris?

383 What, in the Apocrypha, was King Solomon's most famous verdict?

384 What weighing device has the greatest capacity?

385 What translation is regarded as being the greatest, both as art and for being accurate?

386 How well-protected are the vaults of the Federal Reserve Bank in New York?

387 Distinguish among *meteor, meteorite* and *meteorology.*

388 In the anthem "Rule Britannia," what follows the two words of the title in the song?

389 What sort of a vegetable is lichen?

390 Why is a screech owl so called?

391 If you want to test for acidity or alkalinity but have no litmus paper, what can you use instead?

392 Who was the biggest man on record in actual history before 1800?

393 What have the Tasmanian wolf and the hyena in common?

394 Why did the warlike medieval bishops use the mace?

395 Which state touches the greatest number of the Great Lakes?

396 Flotsam is what is lost from a ship that floats, jetsam is what is thrown from a ship; what is lagan?

397 It's said that there is no point in carrying coals to Newcastle. What one-time famous American actually did—and at a great profit—sell coals to that mining town?

398 What caused the origin of "modern" music (sixteenth century to now)?

399 Name the three best conductors of heat.

400 Describe *cleavage* and *brutage*.

401 What is the first thing you would notice about a eucalyptus tree?

402 The addition of *s* at the end of what plural words makes them singular?

403 The nearest star to Earth is Alpha Centauri, which is about 4.3 light years away. Assuming we can travel at the speed of light, what determines the amount of time we would need to reach the star?

404 How many words and phrases, including repeats, can you find in this (one letter words don't count)?
INFACTENOIDEARSIRLOINTIMATEASEND-
INGOTHEM

405 Describe and draw the Chinese abacus, swan pan.

406 Give a palindrome (a word or phrase that spells the same backward and forward) that gives a word for a kind of belief and an example of that kind of belief.

407 What part of the Nile is called the White Nile?

408 What is the object of drag racing?

409 Give the famous acrostic on Charles Lamb (slightly improved).

410 To which are you more closely related, your mother or your sister?

411 What plants, other than the insect-eating pitcher plants, move parts of themselves under their own steam as opposed to growing or being windblown?

412 What kind of seers are not necessarily prophetic?

413 When and by whom was the first balloon sent up?

414 Hermetically sealed now means airtight. What did *hermetically* originally mean?

415 A man planted a lawn enclosed by his house and two straight lines running to an exactly circular pool. Two young friends decided to have a walking race around the lawn, but instead of following the edge of the pool they decided to cut across in a straight line AB making an isosceles triangle with the imaginary point P. At the last moment one said he'd take a longer cross-cut (show-off!), CD. They went at the same speed. Who won, the show-off or his friend?

416 What have the following in common?
Lucie Desmoulins, Elie de Beaumont, Florence of Worcester, Marie Flourens, Anne Girodet de Roussy, Marguerite Elie Gaudet, Maryan Langiewicz, Hyancinthe La Touche, René-Marie Madec, Evangelista Torricelli.

417 What combative-sounding word and its apparent antithesis have the same meaning?

418 What is this?

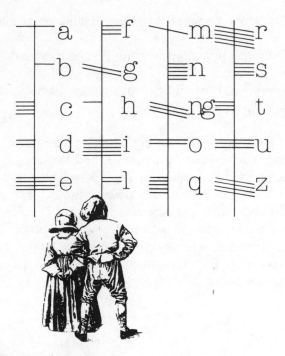

419 What completely imaginary metal is nonetheless useful in certain metallic compounds?

420 What used to be regarded, in school books especially, as the twenty-seventh letter of the alphabet?

421 What, apart from alcohol, were the earliest recorded anaesthetics used in surgery?

422 What form of life is shown here?

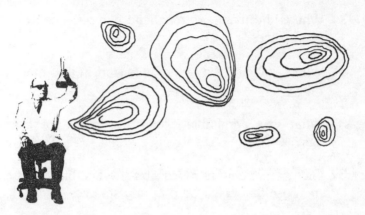

423 How did Solomon digress from monotheism?

424 What invention had the greatest effect on the Old West?

425 What ingenious ploy could be used by a farmer to ensure a fair and equal division of his land between his mutually unfriendly sons on his death?

426 What and where was the first book printed in English?

427 What sentence formed of twelve well-known, frequently used words cannot be written completely?

428 What has Aristophanes done for a U.S. college cheer?

429 What is the country of origin of (a) *gunpowder,* (b) *paper,* (c) *spaghetti?*

430 Who was the world's first (and perhaps most famous) communist?

431 Why is the mariner's magnetic compass inaccurate in most places?

432 When, roughly, did restaurants start in any number in Paris?

433 What was admirable about the real—not Barrie's— Crichton?

434 Give name, date and describe the first bicycle in common use that could be properly steered.

435 Samuel Pepys (1633–1703) wrote a long diary. What period of his life did it cover approximately?

436 What does the word *fresco* mean precisely?

437 What famous magazine ran the same cover design for the longest time?

438 There were flying lizards galore in prehistoric days; are there any around now?

439 Who was the Duke of Exeter's Daughter?

440 Give a rather slangy ancient Irish word we use now and then.

441 Apart from the electric lamp (which he improved but didn't invent), what were Edison's most widely used (in improved form) inventions?

442 Apart from the magnetic compass, what was the first electrical machine and by whom was it invented?

443 Who started carrying the umbrella in England and when?

444 Estimate the approximate area of the United States, not counting Alaska.

445 What was an upholsterer originally (as indicated by his name)?

446 What Latin word is most frequently used in modern English?

447 On what did Karl Marx base his concept of value?

448 We all know that Venice is built on many tiny islands. Which famous city started on one tiny island?

449 What does the term *sterling silver* come from?

450 Who became a saint by merely lending a handkerchief?

451 What, according to their name, should veterinarians confine themselves to treating?

452 François Vidocq was a famous real-life detective. What was a bit odd about him?

453 Describe and name the most repetitive rhyme scheme and verse form.

454 Who is one of the most famous writers of all time and at the same time one whose name we don't know for sure?

455 Describe the first watches (timepieces) carried on the body, the date they were made, and how they were carried.

456 Why do right-handed violinists finger the strings with their left hands when it is so hard to do?

457 How many horns has a rhinoceros?

458 If they are connected, the centers of *any* three circles that touch one another will form a triangle, regardless of the sizes of the circles. An example of this is given in the drawing. (1) Can such triangles be made of any proportion? (2) When the sides X, Y, and Z of a figure are specified, if Z is greater than X + Y, a triangle cannot be made because X and Y cannot meet regardless of the angles. Can this be true in the case of a triangle formed by three circles, and if not, why not?

459 What kind of card game did Gargantua reportedly play?

460 How did James McNeill Whistler evaluate the time taken in making a quick sketch?

461 What do Laplanders call themselves and their country?

462 Of whom, where and when was the first legal electrocution?

463 Which English monarch was in prison prior to becoming sovereign?

464 An Origamian (paperfold expert) couldn't find her square of paper and wanted to establish the length 3″ by folding. Having only a 5″ by 3¾″ rectangle, what did she do? Give proof.

465 In "used," employed, the *s* is pronounced *z*. When can you "use" the same word and pronounce it *s?*

466 At Harvard University there is a famous collection of imitation flowers, all scientifically correct. What are they made of?

467 Who was the first woman painter in Europe to become famous?

468 *For "modern" artists.* How can one paint two lines, red and blue, so that it can't be told from their relative positions and the points at which they overlap which one was done first?

469 Describe what made "Gay rich, and Rich gay."

470 Who was the first Poet Laureate and when was he awarded that honor?

471 Give the simplest example of a Super infinity.

472 In the figure, a and c are parallel, as are b and d, and $\dfrac{a}{b} = \dfrac{c}{d}$. What is the figure called?

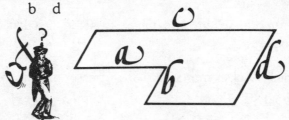

473 Name the biggest invertebrate animal.

474 What is measured with a goneometer?

475 When was the first successful Atlantic cable laid?

476 By what accident and when was the vulcanization of rubber discovered?

477 Who actually first propounded the adage that bad money drives out good?

478 What large country is the narrowest compared with its length?

479 Guido of Arrezo is credited with inventing the first musical notation. He was also the first to use symbols to represent notes of the scale. The first syllables of the words of a hymn to John the Baptist are a mnemonic to memorize the first six notes. Give the verse.

480 Define *tempo* in cookery, and what you do to increase it.

481 How does the total length of Japan compare to the distance from the Canadian border to Brownsville, Texas?

482 Give the name of a black American painter well known in the nineteenth century.

483 Give the title and composer of the song that has the longest melodic line in one continuous uninterrupted stretch in musical history.

484 For what, since there is no recording of his performances, should Richard Tarlton, Elizabeth I's favorite clown, be remembered?

485 What two famous ancient contemporaneous cities had the same name?

486 What physical mathematical problem, important in astronomy, has been proved to be insoluble?

487 Actually how many senses have we in terms of the well-known five (sight, hearing, taste, smell and feeling)?

488 Give the origin and one-time use of the word *treacle*.

489 Apart from making the first steam vehicle, for what is Richard Trevithick known?

490 The phrase "right as a trivet" has been explained by some as being a spoonerism on "tight as a rivet." What is the true basis?

491 Give an example of a word that, unlike *month* or *silver* which have no rhymes, or *horse* which has *course, force,* etc., has only one rhyme. Make the answer poetic, perhaps.

492 Describe how the first printing done in the Middle Ages, long before Gutenberg, differed from his printing.

493 Describe Saint Elmo's fire and relate it to other electrical phenomena.

494 What's wrong with the spelling of *scissors?*

495 The coin collector's son had made a toy pool table and used marbles for balls. He also made a triangular frame for setting them up, but he carelessly made it 5 x 5 x 6 instead of equilateral. He borrowed two of his father's big silver coins and found they fitted exactly onto the wide part of the frame, from which his father was able to calculate the exact size of the coins in his head. How big were they?

496 Describe the first U.S. flag (of the whole country).

497 What has most generally been regarded as the most beautiful building to have been erected since the seventeenth century, perhaps unfairly?

498 What was a *shampoo* at first? What sort of water was used?

499 What people at the beginning of this century were the most numerous in Europe?

500 What article of clothing used by the primitive Stone Age men can be definitely recognized?

501 As an example of how unbelievably sensitive the nose is, how small an amount of what stinky substance can be instantly detected even if not identified by its smell?

502 What English word that ends in *u* is most frequently used?

503 What kind of enormous gem is set in the front of the British crown?

504 What astronomer invented an item that is of great value to architects?

505 Who started the use of penny postage when and on what premise?

506 Mount Everest is the world's highest mountain. What is the second highest?

507 What do these letters stand for and suggest? *Ff*awks; *Ye* (Olde, etc.).

508 An absent-minded archeologist discovered what looked like cuneiform writing; here are the characters below. He couldn't move the wall they were on so he traced them, and when he got home his wife compared the two lines of tracings and got the answer. What did they mean?

509 Time limit: one minute. What letters appear the most frequently in the initials of states of the United States?

510 What astronomical body led to life on land as opposed to marine life on the earth?

511 Who, in nonbiblical times, was said to be (maybe he wasn't) the oldest person on record?

512 How is the name *gringo* for an American suggestive of the song "A partridge in a pear tree"?

513 Who was the first recorded "wild child" (they assumed he had been brought up by wild animals)?

514 What is the main and ever-present constituent of the lead-colored alloy pewter?

515 Who was the first philatelist?

516 What was Joan of Arc's real name?

517 What is the chemical constituent of mammalian bones that gives them their strength?

518 Who actually took the first true photograph, as opposed to a merely sun-stained outline?

519 What did Cristofori invent?

520 What double-named fruit is wrong in both parts of its name?

521 What was unusual about the first or oldest pipe for smoking ever found by Europeans? (American, of course.)

522 How many King Louis's were there in history between Louis I and Louis IV?

523 Why did the early pistols have such a flat angle between the stock and the barrel (see figure)?

524 We all know what a photographer is; what's a phonographer?

525 When and where was the first definitely recorded postal service established (no stamps)?

526 Of what, apart from meters and kilometers, is the centimeter an exactly divisible unit?

527 Considering its origin, what does *proletariat* mean?

528 What did *psalm* mean?

529 When and between whom was the last bare-handed boxing world championship fought?

530 Give as many kinds of queens and their titles and relationships to the crown as you can.

531 What was, we believe, the very first singing commercial on the air in the United States?

532 Here is an English-type crossword puzzle, in which the pattern is one of the clues. Good luck with it.

ACROSS:

1. Brunhilde took it flying.(4)
3. What Adolf promised the Jews, and some took for themselves. (10)
10. One half of America's disgrace, 1927.(5)

11. Tin prisms make the colors off-register.(9)
12. The combination of two towns and a primitive weapon is the root of World War II.(4,6,4)
14. Denoting the lack of a strippeuse's string is how the preacher spoke.(7)
15. 6 down, and pals.(5)
17. Kind of jet, not set—but spinning.(5)
19. To advance would seem to be going for what's in another's eye.(7)
20. Populists, and others who pretend to be.(7,7)
24. Nice, smart, but naughty.(9)
25. This Dame is good at games—ours.(5)
26. To desire an informer in a French island just goes to show.(10)
27. Tax a man from Leith.(4)

DOWN:

1. Fighters in hot storage.(10)
2. *Der Atomic Fuehrer,* they might have called him.(9)
4. The kind we sell abroad is offensive.(5)
5. Where the bell is, over where it should be done.(7)
6. Schicklgruber's right-hand man.(7,7)
7. Out of ten nuisances, one will bore us.(5)
8. An agency the Pentagon doesn't believe.(4)
9. What the French avoided by moving to the country.(7,2,5)
13. The Masses nets a taxable profit.(10)
16. Moses was the first to be.(9)
18. In French, a kind of painting—take a deep breath.(4−3)
21. This car failed in that it stopped selling.(5)
22. Jury or larceny—smallish.(5)
23. *Au secours!* (1,3)

533 In what way was Mary Magdalene censurable?

534 What were the first unidentified flying objects?

535 An inquisitive man had two thick cylindrical rods, parallel and vertical, one 2¼ times the diameter of the other, stuck in a board (see figure). For no reason he stretched a rubber band around the rods and attached a tiny ring at point P of the free part of the band halfway along the part between the two points of contact with the rods, T and T'. The band was near the board at the bottom and he put the point of a pencil through the ring at P and holding it loosely he drew a line outward allowing the tension of the band to guide the point. Describe the line that was drawn.

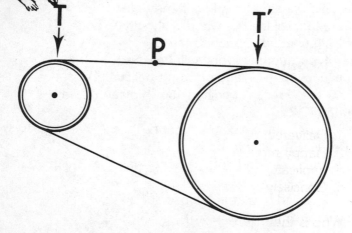

536 What large country has the most complicated legal code?

537 *A Minicrossword puzzle.* English-style diagram, but watch it! (Double trouble . . .)

ACROSS:

1. Two-wheeled vehicle for one passenger.
5. Put a new layer on.
6. Give him what he wants.
7. Woven cloth.

DOWN:

1. Delivered.
2. Happy mountain place in ancient Greece.
3. Implicate.
4. Concisely or succinctly.

538 Who is the most beautiful woman in the world?

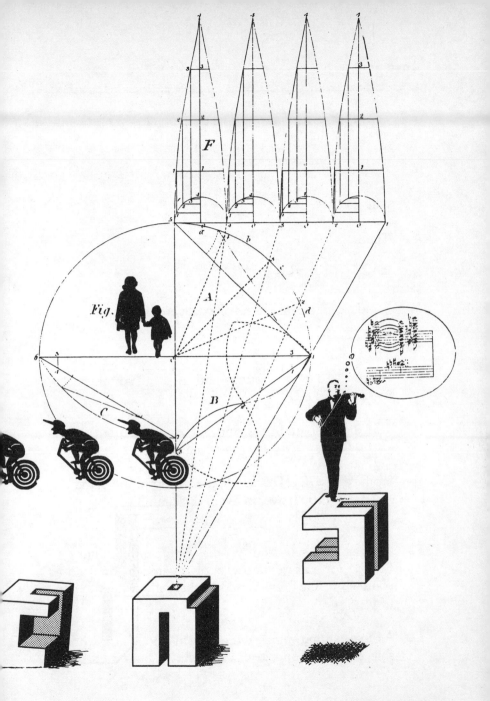

ANSWERS

Answers

1 A river. It is common but its position close to a twenty-story building is not.

2 Adam's rib.

3 A lap.

4 Time.

5 A pair of roller skates.

6 Sunday, when no letters are delivered.

7 PLEAS(E)

8 Saffron. $670 a pound and over. Typical packet weighs 1/16 oz.

9 $\begin{array}{|ccc|} 123 \\ 456 \\ 789 \end{array}$ is one solution that meets the requirements of the question. Easy to remember, too.

Another is $\begin{array}{|ccc|} 672 \\ 159 \\ 834 \end{array}$ This solution adds up to the same answer in every direction.

10 Rubber. It was used in the eighteenth century in Europe for erasers, and was discovered being used as playballs in the New World in the early sixteenth century.

11 All the existing mines were shown, too. Thus, when a ship *didn't* hit one it was thought to be a near miss,

and when a real mine *was* hit it was taken for proof that the map was correct. So German ships tried to avoid all areas shown mined.

12 (a) Drink plenty of fluids. (b) It's for you—it's your answering service. (c) This elevator will self-destruct in five seconds. (d) Take me to the thirteenth floor!

13 In Japan; a number of temples about 2,000 years old.

14 In South England a few flint mines originally used by cavemen now occasionally supply flints for manufacturing the flints for antique guns in museums.

15 On the roads of England, Christmas Eve 1801. Called Road Engine, it was a medium-sized kind of bus driven by a steam engine, made by Richard Trevithick.

16 *Gallia est omnis divisa in partes tres,* or Gaul is all divided in parts three.

17 (a) What hath God wrought? (b) Mr. Watson, come here, I want you. (c) Mary had a little lamb.

18 Not Edison but Pavl Jablochkov, Russian, in 1876. His "electric candle" was the first workable arc light. The first *incandescent* lamp (not a good one) was E. A. King's in 1845 followed by Edison's, the first workable one, in 1879.

19 All of them except (a):
(a) *miniature is from* minium (*the red lead pigment*) *but* miniscule *is from* min (*classical root meaning small*).
(b) *thunder, tendon: from the Sanskrit root* tan, *pull, stretch, resound as a drum*

(c) *hide, cuticle: from Latin* cutis, *skin*
(d) *hen, chanticleer: from Latin* canare, *to sing*
(e) *apricot, precocious: from Latin* praecox, *early ripe*
(f) *water, inundate: from the Indo-Germanic root* wod, *water, which also led to the Greek* hydro

20 At the midnight line, which moves around the Earth opposite the sun.

21 The trick is, and you probably guessed it, that the answers are all in the questions:
(a) *Offhand is* impromptu.
(b) *The next one is its* neighbor.
(c) *An agnostic says he doesn't know.*
(d) *Same has the anagram* mesa.
(e) *Horrible pun;* syzygy *(conjunction of planets) has only* y's.
(f) Giaour *is Turkish for one not believing in Moham- med.*
(g) One word *is an anagram of* new door.

22 None. Petard (or *petar* in Shakespeare) is a small bomb.

23 It circulates the hot air that stoves give off. Fireplaces (non-smoking ones) only give off radiant heat; un- blowable.

24 A base of earth: a *pleasance* is a pleasure garden, and a *ha ha* is a sunken fence or ditch or both.

25 The title deed to a piece of monastery land. The abbot of the monastery sent the deed to John Horner hidden away in a pie and smuggled past the Tudor troops as part of the customary holiday gifts of food to the poor.

It was hoped that, once Henry VIII's campaign against the Church had ended, the deed would enable him to return the land to the monastery. However, the monastery was abolished, and Horner kept the land for himself, an outcome which casts some doubts on his original reasons for entering into the plot. Like many nursery rhymes, the story of Little Jack Horner refers to real events—the Horners owned a certain piece of ex-church land as recently as fifty years ago.

26 An ancient feast still occasionally given by the Printers' Guild in England and other printers.

27 Red, *green* and *violet:* the true primaries applied to colored light. Red, yellow and blue primaries apply to pigments, in which we get green by mixing yellow and blue, etc., but with lights we get yellow by mixing red and green, and blue by mixing green and violet.

28 Krakatao, an island near Java, August 1883. The waves caused by this eruption killed more than 30,000 people.

29 (a) dentistry, (b) younger, (c) science of homebrewing, (d) cobbler, (e) cotton, (f) murder.

30 That of detecting the presence of a base metallic substitute in the king's gold crown, by comparing specific gravities. The method is to weigh the object that is supposedly gold in air, then under water. The ratio between these weights is then compared to that of known gold.

31 Heard, herd, bird, word, curd.

33   The first list is a list of letters in order of frequency of use in English. The second list is the order of their use as initial letters. So *e* is the most frequently used letter in English, *t* is next, etc. But more words begin with *s* than any other letter, then *c,* etc.

34   Using the symbol for factorial, ! , and then defining n! as simply n((n = 1)!):
Substitute $n = 1$
then $1! = 1((1-1)!)$
(a) $1 = 1 \times 0!$
(b) $\underline{1 = 0!}$

But substitute $n = 0$
then $0! = 0((0-1)!)$
                           $0! = 0$
thus from (a) $1 = 0! = 0$
therefore $1 = 0.$

Your math teacher might point out that $(-1)!$ doesn't exist or that $0!$ is arbitrarily defined as 1—but it does look pretty convincing, doesn't it?

35 *The Mirror.* It does neither (as if you didn't know!)—it reverses you back-to-front. If you walk up to a full-length mirror, your face will touch your reflected face, toes touch toes and also your right hand will touch your reflected right hand and same with left. Now, hold on; your front may be against "your" front, and back away from back, *but* according to the compass your right hand is on the east side, your left on the west, head up and feet down, and the same with the reflections, except that *you*'re facing north and the reflection faces south, i.e., like the spherical mirror, which you can turn top-to-bottom, but not back-to-front. All this shows that the only reason we think we're reflected as changed left-to-right and not top-to-bottom is really based on our usual manner of turning back-to-front. If *we* were facing south like the reflection and then we turned around to the mirror not keeping upright but flopping over vertically (horizontal axis) with head down at the end, we'd find the mirror had reversed our top (our left hand) with our bottom (right hand), and not our left (head) with our right (foot). Thus it's only due to our normal left-to-right way of turning back-to-front, which the mirror has symmetrically done for us. The same would happen if we had a rubber glove, fingers away from us, on a table; if we turn it inside-out without otherwise moving it, thumb would remain on the east side and palm on top, but fingers now toward us.

36 They were all born in the same year—1856.

37 No change. Everything falls at the same speed, and gravity is the sole cause of the pendulum's downward motion, m.

39 Hessian.

40 Bethlehem's is 25,000 to Nantucket's 3,000.

41 Across 1 and 3, Down 1 and 2—all four words are *exclamations.*

42 They would both rust. The hawk Hamlet meant is an iron pallet with a wooden handle, used to hold mortar—not a bird.

43 It is upside down.

44 In the General Prologue to the Wycliffe translation of the Bible, 1384. (*See* Bartlett's *Familiar Quotations.*)

45 Alarm clocks or timepieces with second hands. Should be called third hands!

46 They are all stitches.

47 Raw egg white. (It was used as a medium in many medieval paintings.)

48 By sentencing both to life imprisonment. There is no innocent one. The non-murderer is guilty of the crime of protecting—by not testifying against—the murderer, a crime equal to murder in the eyes of the law.

49 BOMB
TOMB
COMB

50 It would not cool the kitchen at all; in fact, it would heat the kitchen very slightly. In a refrigerator the heat is removed from the inside and transferred to the outside (the kitchen). The net result is a slight increase because of the energy expended to do so.

51 In the late nineteenth century, as an adjunct to women's underwear, corsets, etc., as fasteners. It was revived during World War I, at first merely for tobacco pouches, when it became known as a Zipper.

52 Autobiography.

53 Hold your hand in the position shown to the left below. Then spread your fingers as shown, and move the two in the middle back again without moving the others.

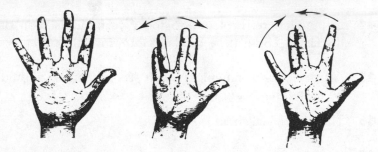

54 You and I are both different from Jones, but you are more different than I am.

55 The movement of standing on one's toes, or raising the knees when sitting. In the latter case you can lift a very heavy person sitting on your knees with very little sense of strain compared to what you would feel when lifting him with your arms. The calf muscles seem to be the most powerful and efficient in the human body.

56 Blinking is so fast that it leaves no after impression of visible movement as opening does. It may be a safety device to protect the eyes.

57 Apparently, within limits, the longer the easier, although since technically speaking a very small change of order of letters gives an anagram, then theoretically one may have an unlimited part of the original unaltered. For example, "like the symbols for *e* and *o* . . ." can be changed to "like the symbols for *o* and *e*" giving an "anagram." Try "Now is the time for all good men to come to the aid of the party." Answer: "Come, why at the total time limit do poor oaf-men get hired so often?"

58 K, as in know, knee, knot, etc.

59 Read it out loud and you'll hear the numbers from 1 to 10.

60 A is already boiling. Further heating will merely reduce its quantity without raising its temperature, so there will be less to mix with B.

61

62 Red. If honestly run, the chances are normally even, but a run of nineteen means the wheel may be out of order and tend toward red.

63 It has one hump and would normally be called a dromedary.

64 An armchair.

65 Cop B is more venal because he can be bought more easily; but according to the Bible, I Timothy 6:9 and 10, A is more wicked since he is after more money. Take your choice.

66 At the center of the earth, if so deep a mine were ever dug.

68 Press A down hard and with the other hand slide a third quarter C against it. B will jump away, leaving room for the dime. Like this:

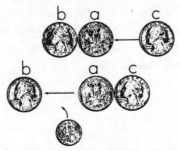

69 Normal temperature of the human body (98.6° Fahrenheit).

70 By similar triangles, since CEGD is a square, CE is parallel to BF, and CAE is equilateral, AC = CE = DC. Draw AG ⊥ CE; by symmetry GC = ½CE = ½ AC, by similar triangles CB = 2BD. Let BD = 1, then BC = 2 and

CD $= \sqrt{3} =$ AC, by the Pythagorean theorem. Then if AB $= 1$, CD $= \dfrac{\sqrt{3}}{2+\sqrt{3}}$

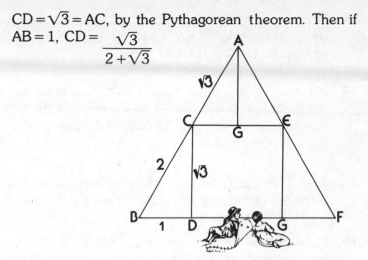

71 No glass. They were made of polished steel or silver.

72 $\sqrt{3}/2$. Proof: mentally bisect AB at C, join PB and PC. PB is radius of arc A, as is AB so AB $=$ PB $= 1$. Double the scale of figure: PCB is a right triangle with hypotenuse PB $= 2$ and base CB $= 1$. Since $2^2 + 1^2 = 3$, PC $= \sqrt{3}$, by the Pythagorean Theorem. Thus in original scale $h = \sqrt{3}/2$. Q.E.D.

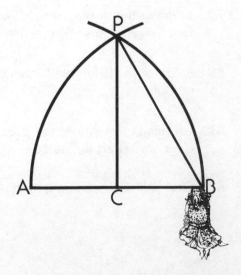

73 Because its ore was mistakenly thought to contain copper, and the original German name was *Kupfernickel,* or Copper Demon (cf. Old Nick).

74 No one. An unknown woman said "Let them eat brioche" (a non-sweet roll). It was not Marie Antoinette. See Rousseau quoted in Bartlett's *Familiar Quotations,* from his *Confessions.*

75 Tripoli, in 1801, because of the American attitude toward the piracy Tripoli's government condoned.

76 He was a black man who with Robert E. Peary and four Eskimos was the first to reach the North Pole.

77 A Haughty Spirit. (Pride goeth before destruction.) Prov. 16:18.

78 The Bible says he was 969. One modern theory is that the Old Testament years were what we call months, so he was 80 years 9 months.

79 In riding the front wheel follows a more wiggly, therefore longer, course (in steering, etc.) than the rear one.

80 Salerno in Italy, ninth century—chiefly a medical school.

81 Learning, not knowledge. Alexander Pope, "Essay on Criticism" (Part II, line 15).

82 One half. If the beam is rotated to the position shown here we see that its corners touch the sides of the hole. Its four quarters equal the open space. Q.E.D.

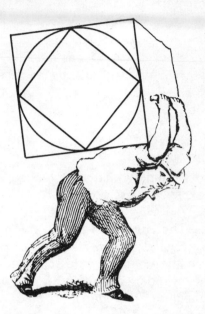

83 Henry Carey (1687–1743). The two invented words are *aldiborontiphoscophornio* and *chrononhoton-thologos,* from the play of the latter name.

84 Because ten is only divisible by 1, 2 and 5, whereas twelve is divisible by 1, 2, 3, 4, and 6. (*Duodecimal* means based on 12.)

85 No miles. It is nearly 100 miles farther east than Reno.

86 Not Brownsville, Texas, but Boca Grande key near Key West, Florida.

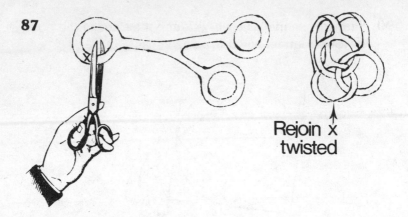

Rejoin x twisted

88 Villager, boy, unknown, straight, twisted, breath, child of either sex, speechless one.

89 Two inches. The volume of a cone is $\frac{1}{3}\pi r^2 h$ while the volume of a cylinder is $\pi r^2 h$, i.e., just three times as much. Since the volume of this cone equals the volume of the cylinder 1″ high and the diameters are equal, the height of the cone must be 3″ and thus the part above the rim, 2″.

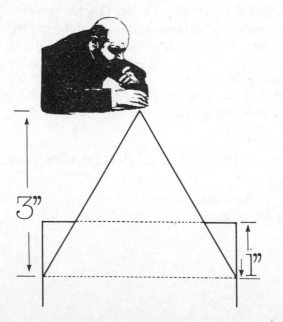

90 François Marie Arouet, Josef Korzeniowski, Jacques Thibault.

91 Refuse.

92 Because we see all of a given pole at once, whereas the drops are moving from top to bottom.

93 Massachusetts, Plymouth, Connecticut and New Haven. They were more usually called the New England Confederacy by outsiders.

94 The *Oxford Gazette*, 1665, which was published at irregular intervals.

95 The *Acta Diurna*, Rome, second century. Juvenal said that the ladies used to spend the morning reading it.

96 California redwood trees.

97 The modern whales, much larger than the biggest dinosaurs.

98 An iron chain is wrapped around its base.

99 The fact that the Arabic has a symbol for zero.

100 The discovery of a cave painting showing a Victorian lady and a top-hatted gentleman in a horse-drawn carriage.

101 NEEDLE(SS).

102 It is not a horn, but a woodwind. The basset (which is a kind of clarinet) was invented by a Mr. Horn.

103 A tinker fixed holes in pots and pans. He used a dam of clay to hold the solder that he mended them with in place. It was thrown away when the solder dried, and so was not worth much.

104 Just keep repeating *toy boat, toy boat,* ad inf.

105 It is parallel to one side, between it and the center.

106 The lightning rod, bifocal lenses and the Franklin stove.

107 The number written out in full would not go in this book.

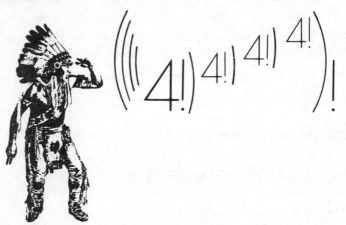

108 A sundial.

109 An hourglass timer with its uncounted grains of sand.

110 The compass (it's electromagnetic).

111 In being the first known English poem (not in continental Anglo-Saxon), the first known English piece of music and the first known round, or canon. Also it is in seven parts (very rare) and the style is far ahead of its time, almost Renaissance. Words and music probably by John of Fornsete, c. 1250.

> *Sumer is icumen in,*
> *Lhude sing cuccu!*
> *Groweth sed and bloweth med,*
> *And springth the wude nu—*
> *Sing cuccu!*

112 Apparently for easier export of wine. The chief original market was England—where it was to be mixed with soda water, thus in a way remaking it into the sparkling wine from which it was distilled.

113 Salt; sodium chloride, found chiefly in the sea.

114 Guard (Old High German *guard peace*). They were originally watchtowers.

115 Most people think it is MIX; MID is still bigger.

116 Sir Moses Montifiore, 1784—1885.

117 Put a big block of ice in a pan on the floor, and turn an electric fan on it. Shut the windows. It works.

118 Scotland, near Glasgow, early in the century. Many people in London and even the United States used to send their clothes there to be cleaned.

119 Because they were photographed at a lower rate of speed than talkies or TV, so that modern projectors and especially TV exhibit them much faster than was intended. Only a few theaters like the Museum of Modern Art, New York, use the correct projectors nowadays.

120 A roll of paper towel, measuring approximately 140 sq. ft. The perforations leave it in one piece. Newspapers are far smaller per sheet and the large posters are correctly called 24-sheet (separate), each about 3' by 4'. The average person never sees full newsprint rolls.

121 At one time barbers were surgeons in general practice as well as cutters of hair and shavers of chins. The design represented bloody bandages. Henry VIII seems to have passed an edict that barbers could not practice surgery (except bloodletting) and surgeons could not shave people.

122 It is named after the famous singer Dame Nellie Melba—real name Helen Mitchell—who took her name from her birthplace, Melbourne, Australia, which was named after Lord William Melbourne.

123 *First* open all windows and exterior doors; a tornado is a partial vacuum which will suck them open if they are closed. Then disconnect the electricity, put out *every* fire and turn off all gas pilots. Then go to the storm cellar.

124 Smell. Light, sound, pressure and taste are pretty well explained, but how does the nose almost instantly analyze and recognize such tiny quantities of such a huge number of subtly complex compounds? We only *taste* four: bitter, sweet, sour and salt.

125 (a) slate; (b) vulcanized rubber; (c) celluloid; (d) glass (air-filled); (e) red phosphorus; (f) platinum; (g) coal, air and water; (h) parchment.

126 4 by 13 cards, measuring 12″ by 26″; 2, 4 and 13 are the only divisors of 52.

127 Vegetable.

128 Spanish, imported to India by, of all people, the Portuguese.

129 Bagpipe music, as given by the verbal equivalents, instead of regular musical notation. In a way it resembles *solfeggio,* do re mi fa sol la ti do, but it also gives the rhythm.

130 The rectangle R has been transposed to R′ and the dividing line PP′ is the required one. The transposition has no effect on the areas involved. The proof is evident.

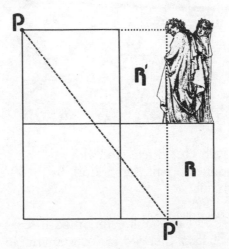

131 *Pasta:* macaroni, spaghetti, noodles, etc.

132 Rook in 15 moves in a square spiral toward the center. Queen takes 15, rook's pawn 19 by queening, Bishop can't. See fig. below.

133 People with breath expelled almost float, so they measure about one pint per pound, i.e., 160 pints, or 20 gallons in all.

134 In A.D. 330 Constantine renamed it first New Rome, which was later changed to Constantinople, although it continued to be known to many as Byzantium. In modern times it became Istanbul.

135 The early science-fictions of Swift and Poe. The real Cyrano, who was a seventeenth-century French poet, wrote light-hearted science romances about the sun and moon.

136 Fly.

137 Not the discovery of America, as the news wouldn't have reached London that year. Most likely the expulsion of the Moors from Spain.

138 Fur. In translation, Perrault's *verre*, glass, was a misreading of *vair*, fur.

139 A: segment, B: sector, D: lune.

140 Brazil. More than twice the size of any other.

141 Rely.

142 *What ho!* spelled *Hwat ho.*

143 The phrase is from Pope's eighteenth-century translation of Homer's Greek original.

144 Fourteenth-century conjurers, mentioned by Chaucer, are the first we know of. Some experimental talkies were made before 1910 (Encycl. Brit., 11th Ed.).

145 The Susan Constant, the God Speed and an unnamed pinnace.

146 Muang Thai, Sibir.

147 Singer, Metropolitan Life and Woolworth Buildings.

148 Orpheus, who kept his crew from listening to the Sirens by loudly playing his lyre.

149 Thinking that *either* should be pronounced *eyether;* the U.S. is the older and right version as the later, and current, English one was started when the German George I mispronounced *ei* in the German way, which was immediately copied by the upper crust.

150 The air-cushion effect of narrowing the shaft. It is self-activating, thus automatic.

151 Socrates, 470–399 B.C.

152 Obviously, Arabic numerals won't be used (10, 11, 12), but III, VII, VIII and XII (also the fairly frequent old-time IIII).

153 Ireland: the Culdees.

154 England to the west of Brighton on the south coast. Planted by the first Prince Regent in the early nineteenth century, and still there.

155 You don't; for best results turn it over and tear the envelope carefully off *it.*

156 I Kings 7:23. "And he made a moulten sea, ten cubits from the one brim to the other, it was round all about . . . and a line of thirty cubits did compass it round about."

157 Utter rubbish as a means of judging intelligence. Even if relative sizes of a brain were reliable indications, the shape can vary without any effect on the volume. The Facial Angle is the angle between the lines *aa* and *bb* in the figure—it varies enormously in man. The Cephalic Index is the ratio of the maximum width to the maximum length of a skull, multiplied by 100.

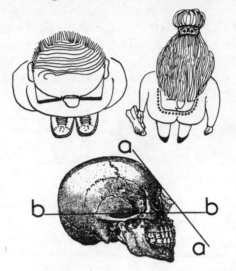

158 The Old Glory. In 1831, when Captain William Driver was given the flag in recognition for "humanity in taking back some of the Bounty mutineers to their former home on Pitcairn Island," he so named it.

159 Aeaea, Circe's island.

160 Not the peregrine falcon, as is usually thought, but the humming bird, who goes fast enough to harass a diving eagle.

161 Because of Esq.

162 The products that we call "mineral oil" are all eventually derived from carbon compounds, organic, not mineral.

163 The sound gets fainter but it does not lower in pitch as it should according to the Doppler effect—his speed increases in falling, thus the frequency lessens.

164 Fold as shown, each time making a tight angle with the previous edge folded. The process can be carried out indefinitely.

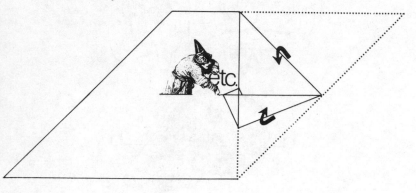

165 ETATS (French for *states*).

166 Ambergris, a morbid secretion of sperm whales, found floating in the sea.

167 Wagner; he wrote them himself.

168 That many scientists are very gullible; it was a fake.

169 See figure. Note that the cutting edge is straight and not bent at the tip, so the knife doesn't pull the already cut pieces toward you but leaves them in position. Very useful in cross-cutting or dicing.

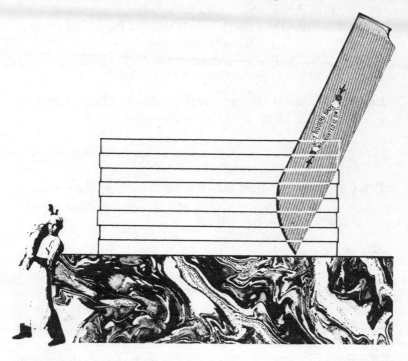

170 "See you on the lynx!"

171 Wait, get your strength back and try just once more—you've probably already loosened it and it needed a moment to think things over.

172 One of the strands of the Atlantic, or perhaps the Pacific cable. Land telephone and power lines are in sections that are merely brought together into electrical contact temporarily when needed.

173 REPROBATE Scoundrel, from Latin *repugnans,*
repugnant
PROBATE Will, from Latin *probatus,* proved
BATE Lower (one's breath) from Old French
abatre, beat down
ATE Consumed, from Anglo-Saxon *etan,* eat.

174 The kinkajou, an arboreal South American mammal which can climb up its own (prehensile) tail.

175 A lost band (of men); from the Dutch *verolen hoop.*

176 For those non-nest-building birds that lay their eggs on rock ledges, the conical shape makes the eggs roll in a circle and thus not fall off.

177 The rhythm given, for example, by the words "*Shave* and a haircut, sham*poo,*" or the English "*Tripe* and bananas, stewed *fruit.*" Just the rhythm in the Morse code: − · · − − pause − − is recognizable without either musical notes or words. We believe it is unique.

178 Both were insults: the Puritans, contrary to the prevailing fashion of long-haired men, cut theirs short and were referred to derisively as Roundheads (like our Rednecks); the supporters of the King had long hair, but were referred to as Cavaliers, or servants (i.e., to the King).

179 The burning of one of the Nine Wonders of the World, the Alexandrian Library.

180 Wedgwood's porcelain was chiefly famous for the delicately molded figures by John Flaxman, sculptor, that adorned it.

181 Iceland. They did have a somewhat democratic form of government under Denmark's kings, to whom they gave allegiance until this century.

182 No actual picture is made of it except on the TV screen, where it is evanescent. The recording on tape is a linear message or code, not a recognizable picture.

183 Not later, but one year earlier, in 1610.

184 OUR becomes YOUR.

185 When hospitalized he is no longer the doctor but the patient.

186 It is the initial letters of the months.

187 Calling it an insect. A spider is an arachnid.

188 The word *bosh* is Turkish.

189 Move to another place where you will not be allowed to vote for a year and plead or claim unfair to tax without representation.

190 Indiana (Chicago is in Illinois).

191 Their intention was to free ballet and opera respectively from the Italian conventions, which were thought to be old-fashioned.

192 The bristlecone pine tree.

193 No recognizable echo, but the loudness would be doubled.

194 Steel's tensile strength is greater provided the rods are thick enough. When the diameter is less than a certain size, depending on the type of steel, the same size of nylon thread or filament is stronger. Nylon is not crystalline.

195 Wild "rice" is not rice but marsh grass seed.

196 Solicitors, in law, are not supposed to solicit business; if they do they are called "ambulance chasers."

197 Sweden, developed in the mid-nineteenth century, taken to Russia where it modified the Italian ballet and melded to some extent with the Russian folk dancing before it reached its final form.

198 A *solecism* is a minor blunder in speech; *solipsism* is the philosophical belief that the self can only know itself.

199 The number left in the dish has no bearing on who ate how many; A could have been right if he had been keeping count.

200 A "round" web is not truly round; the outer rim is a polygon and is made first, then the radii and last a continuous spiral is laid out, not concentric circles.

201 Lever, inclined plane, wheel and axle, screw, pulley, wedge.

202 Very rarely over twenty miles. Usually about ten or twelve.

203 Four. For example, as the diagram shows, the ground-level wind is from the west; the low with accompanying rain moves east, but first gives movement of the cloud cover to the north, then to the south. Meanwhile the jet stream very high up is bringing over a warm, dry front from the northwest.

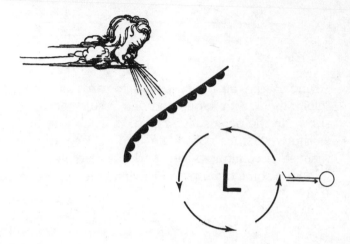

204 From a sheet of typewriter paper cut out the pattern shown in Figure 1 being sure to carry the cut line indicated by C beyond the fold line. Then cut the piece in two as shown, and fold the right-hand loop over to the left.

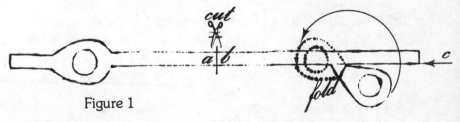

Figure 1

Next, as shown in Figure 2, slide the two parts together, with end A going on top of B, and bring B through the left-hand loop and A through the right-hand loop. When the loops are a little closer, the ends

Figure 2

A and B can be bent up and towards one another; rejoin them with tape, and the result should be as shown in the perspective Figure 3. Then pull the ends as shown; first the right-hand loop will be torn from the main strip; continue pulling and the main piece will tear in two at some other point, leaving you with three fragments.

Figure 3

205 Dactylology, the signs made with the fingers indicating the letters of the alphabet.

206 An old-fashioned fountain pen—*not* ball-point—which tends to make ink blobs when a low is coming over. Also sharpening a pencil with a knife; in dry weather the chips stick to the knife and the paper.

207 In Edinburgh, Scotland in 1771, by a group of Scottish men. The editor was William Smellie.

208 Twelfthtide.

209

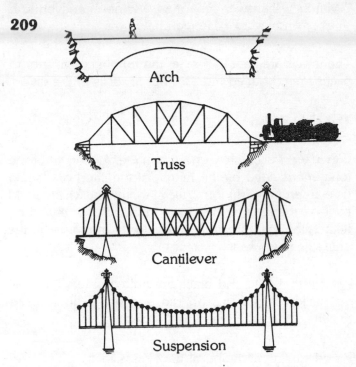

Arch

Truss

Cantilever

Suspension

210 Er, you know, well, I mean, etc. The first meaning of the word *expletive* is "something added merely as a filler." "Oath" is second meaning.

211 Pencil sharpening.

212 A colony of Albanis, of all places. See Livy, lib. I, Cap. XXII.

213 A non-sweet honey-flavored beer. Slightly sour as a rule, and fizzy. If sweet, it has not yet matured. (Made from honey.)

214 Say "Yes-or-no." Then the judge crossly says, "Witness will answer yes, or answer no!" and you say, "Yes or answer no." Heaven help you.

215 The jewels are kept in a safe; the numbers refer not to paces to find buried treasure but to turns of the dial.

216 The Holy Bible.

217 If they were accurately enough made, the length of the long one divided by the length of the short one could give an enormously long decimal number which could code *all* the facts at this given moment of every atom, its position and direction and velocity of motion in the entire finite universe.

218 Pointillism. White and black are not considered as colors; yellow is gotten with red and green dots mixed together; blue with green and violet.

219 President. Count the number of assassinations and see.

220 Only four: sweet, sour, salt and bitter. All the countless others are detected by the nose. Try holding your nose when you have some taste like, say, tomatoes in your mouth: you will taste salt, a faint sourness and a slight sweetness—nothing else.

221 Lie-abed.

222 "Is" is a copulative verb, and so is "to be," so ask him if he would say, "How would you like to be I for a day?"

223 Seven rows: eight in the second and sixth, seven in the rest as shown.

224 That he is numb. If he is sick he should say "I feel *bad*."

225 A north wind isn't going north, as a north road is, it's coming from the north.

226 Its initials comprise the alphabet.

227 See figures. Note that there are surprising gaps that occur in the spiral; the lengths go 1, 3, 5, 7, etc.

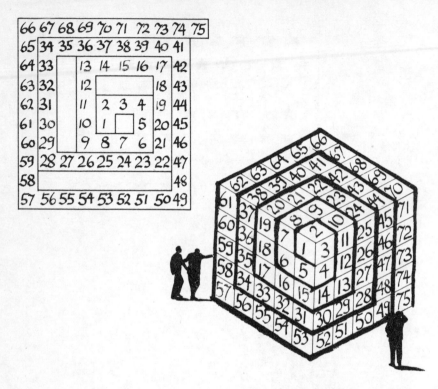

228 Give the catalog to sit on, sing the catastrophe, let the catamount to something, in every categorical detail.

229 Michigan.

230 In Irvine, Scotland. He next attended a boarding school in Chelsea, and in 1817 became a student at the Manor House School in Stoke Newington, England. He then returned to America. He wrote one short novel, *The Narrative of Arthur Gordon Pym* of Nantucket.

231 From the Channel Island French, "Haru! Haru! Viens à mon aide, mon seigneur, on me fait tort!" called out by hereditary right when they wanted legal protection. No one knows why or how the circus people took it up, but they did use it as a warning to one another when a dangerous person was present.

232 Aluminum. (The tip of the Washington Monument is made of it.)

233 Answer: 8. In some mathematics *i* means to turn at right angles.

234 The north shore of Lake Erie is the southernmost edge of Canada It is level with northern Connecticut.

235 Beethoven's (unfinished) Tenth Symphony. The clues are that it sounds like Beethoven, and being orchestral, if you are musically well-read you will realize it is not part of any of his known works; thus it must be part of the scherzo of his Tenth.

236 Skiing.

237 The paper is cut in a spiral that gets narrower as it approaches the edge, which is a circle to which the spiral is asymptotic. Its area and weight are finite, naturally. Try making one. The thing should be endless, but that is of course impossible.

238 Zero. His center of gravity would be in orbit considering speed of rotation of the earth. Sumatra is on the Equator.

239 The word *answer.*

240 Greenland Eskimo language for, "He says that you also will go away quickly in like manner and buy a pretty knife!" (One word!) (See Encyclopedia Britannica, eleventh ed., Vol. ix, p. 70.)

241 Schumann had a peculiar difficulty in raising one of the fingers of his right hand when the neighboring fingers were held down. He pulled on it and permanently damaged the muscle so he had to give up virtuoso concertizing and applied himself seriously to composition.

242 The three most frequently used letters, *e, t* and *a,* are struck by the left hand.

243 Exactly one.

244 Politics.

245 Anthony Clement McAuliffe replying "Nuts!" to a German ultimatum, World War II.

246 "Damn the torpedoes! Captain Drayton, go ahead! Jouett, full speed!" (See Bartlett's *Familiar Quotations.*)

247 The ocarina. The pitch in mouth whistling.

248 Nodding and shaking the head.

249 Pandora.

250 Saint Linus (A.D. 67?–?79).

251 Lutetia.

252 A great temple to Jupiter built during the Roman occupation of Gaul.

253 They don't exist. What we call spiral staircases are helical.

254 When applied to an elderly man or woman we say "ajed," but when speaking of a man or woman of forty-five or so we say "middle-aged" and the last part is really one syllable.

255 It isn't. The word comes from Latin *mola,* cereal grits mixed with salt and put on what is sacrificed.

256 Mozart. It is true that Hitler was a house painter, but any true artist in any field is more likely to be good at any art than a non-artist. In fact in the Renaissance most artists tried their hand at most arts, not to mention science.

257 Mathematics. He was called *Khayyám* (tentmaker in Persian) probably because of his father's occupation, one which he followed only in his youth.

258 Ladoga, U.S.S.R.

259 China, in 1729.

260 The drops from it form what amounts to a stalagmite

with which it eventually fuses and which then supports it.

261 Since the light would hardly be over the center of the pool, the latter is probably elliptical. Since the light was partially shaded (it did not shine in all directions) it produced a cone, of which the ellipse is a section.

262 An Atlantic island, part of France.

263 North-central Minnesota.

264 Christopher Wren, the architect.

265 The tall man on the short, as he will certainly have longer arms.

266 According to inscriptions at Karnak, in the time of Seti I, c. 1380 B.C., a canal of sorts connected the Nile with the Red Sea. Lesseps, who engineered the modern one, didn't get going until the mid-nineteenth century.

267 A grand piano.

268 Scottish. Alexander Graham Bell moved to Boston, Massachusetts, from Scotland.

269 This is the rebus of *rebus:*

270 Zero; it appears only nine times, as compared to the rest, which are used twenty times each.

271 Coming up too fast, because of the dissolving of nitrogen in the blood. When the swimmer reaches the surface, the nitrogen comes out of solution, forming bubbles which may cause heart stoppage.

272 The conductor's baton, and in rare cases the tambourine when it is merely shaken as a sistrum.

273 A slate pencil.

274 By drawing wiggly lines parallel to the coast line, which will be recognizable when photographically reproduced. Also sometimes by putting imaginary islands in.

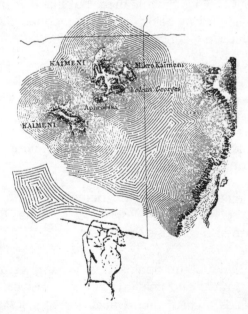

275 Animal.

276 Stethoscope, where it means examine by hearing.

277 Blood, Phlegm, Choler and Melancholy.

278 Point Barrow, Alaska.

279 His height. According to legend he was nearly 6' 4'', an unusual height for his era.

280 Facetiously.

281 $1x \dfrac{(9-8) + (7-6)}{(5-4) + (3-2)}$

282 Noah's ark. Don't forget the elephants, hippos, etc.

283 Other buildings have leaned, but this one started leaning while it was being built and they went right ahead without straightening it.

284 The Statue of Liberty.

285 They are all grasslands but the Veldt has occasional trees, while the others supposedly do not.

286 Less than two feet. The islands are in your middle and the canals in your ears.

287 The initial letters give the notes, in C major, of "My Country, 'Tis of Thee," or "God Save the Queen." The rhythm also suggests the music.

288 The Riddle of the Sphinx was: What goes on four legs, then on two and finally on three? Answer: A man; he crawls as a child, then walks and at last walks with a stick.

289 About half as tall, approximately 500 feet.

290 For having allegedly taken part in the conspiracies against James I. He was under sentence of death for fifteen years before he finally was executed.

291 Ramie is a plant which produces a strong fiber. Prior to the introduction of plastic yarns like nylon and the like, it was of unequaled tensile strength.

292 By painting the highlights. The background went on last.

293 A type of flat sea fish (that can kill with the current it produces). It doesn't go anywhere near 10,000 mph.

294 It is a vine.

295 The old carpenters' caps were rectangular boxes; see Tenniel's illustrations of the Carpenter in *Alice in Wonderland*. (Try folding one out of paper.)

296 *Dafne,* 1597, Jacopo Peri, of Florence, Italy.

297 1840, in England.

298 Two pounds. Imagine the cut piece to be divided down the dotted line, and then put together as shown; it will be a cylinder one-fifth the total length.

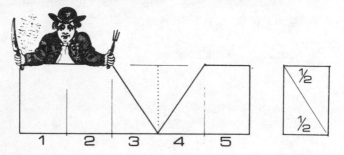

299 For generating acid (Greek *oxys*).

300 Successively multiplying the whole numbers: $0 \times 1 = 0$, $1 \times 2 = 2$, $2 \times 3 = 6$, $3 \times 4 = 12$, $4 \times 5 = 20$, $5 \times 6 = 30$, etc.

301 The Christians.

302 For raising water by suction. (Watt greatly improved the steam engine. He didn't invent it.)

303 With his toes.

304 At once start a brush fire to your south which will burn away before the main fire reaches you, giving you a cleared-out space which the fire cannot cross, as there is no brush there left to burn. When it's all out, walk to the north end.

305 In inactive volcanoes.

306 He fell out of bed—presumably a very high one.

307 Boston.

308 Aristarchus, in Greece, c. 250 B.C.

309 Helmets.

310 George Eliot and George Sand (both pen names).

311 Sarah Bernhardt, in 1899. (She was more famous than the male actors.)

312 The Andes, about 4,400 miles.

313 It is the only really big river that flows north.

314 He was against it; in fact there is only one recorded instance of his having imposed it and he regretted it so much that he did penance for it. His sons had very different views.

315 A ten-letter word, say *everywhere* (count the others).

316 A *catastrophe* is a turning over, or disaster; a *cataclysm* is a flood or deluge.

317 Mainly of sheep. The confusion of the old name *kit* for fiddle has led to the common error of thinking they're strung with the intestines of cats.

318 The letter *e* is not used. (It usually is the most frequently used letter in English.)

319 African goliath beetles and the U.S. elephant beetles.

320 Cover a piece of paper with white watercolor paint—a ball of cloth will do to spread the paint. When it's dry you can draw on it with the tine of a silver fork. This process is called silverpoint.

321 He was an able astronomer and mathematician. He was *not* a pirate as so many people believe now; perhaps he has been confused with J. M. Barrie's Captain Hook?

322

323 100,000 rupees, Indian. No lack there.

324 Frozen dew.

325 One and a third pounds.

326 The dulcimer.

327 We can make a drypoint by scratching the design on a celluloid triangle with the point of a compass. No press is necessary as slightly damp paper can be placed on the freshly inked and wiped surface and rubbed on the back with a fingernail.

328 The first is a euphemism (the substitution of a mild, inoffensive expression for an unpleasant one), the second a sort of euphuism (artificial elegance of language, from John Lyly's "Euphues").

329 The month of February, because the cabbage came up then.

330 The composition of music. He is not to be confused with Leonardo da Vinci, 1452–1519. He lived from 1690 to 1730.

331 *Officiers de police,* not *gendarmes,* who are quasi-military police.

332 He first showed great musical skill, then decided he wanted to be a painter, but he was brought up to be a medical doctor. He became fascinated by mathematics and against his father's will studied it and became a physicist.

333 Fill it with smoke. (The word means "to disinfect with smoke, etc.")

334 The western borders of Colorado and New Mexico; not the Canadian border as that is a parallel of latitude, not a great circle.

335 First, real Gruyère cheese, which is made in Gruyère in

Switzerland, has very small holes and not many of them. What we get instead doesn't come from there as the home product is practically all eaten in the vicinity. What you get when you order it in a city even so close to Gruyère as Geneva is probably Ementhaler.

336 In no play; she is merely referred to by another character in Morton's play *Speed the Plough* (1798).

337 1,000 miles, approximately, which is nearly four times the length of the United Kingdom.

338 Enough untaxed land was discovered to more than compensate for the cost. In many cases land areas had been grossly underestimated and since land is usually taxed by the acre, these untaxed acres justified tax increases.

339 MANSLAUGHTER for MANS LAUGHTER.

340 A *shambles* is a place of slaughter, thus with blood all over everything; a *holocaust* is destruction by fire (c.f. *caustic*).

341 The Irish were there around A.D. 850, before the Scandinavians.

342 Oxford. Bosporus is Greek for "Oxen's ford."

343

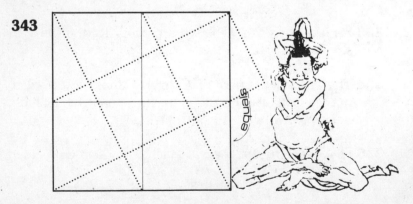

344 Very sleepy, it contains a mild soporific. (Remember Peter Rabbit.)

345 1829, supposedly invented by Isaac Holden.

346 Voyage (from French *voyer*) means to go and look; journey (French *jour*) is a day's trip.

347 According to rabbinical mythology he first married Lilith, an evil spirit. In the Middle Ages she was regarded as a witch.

348 It is itself redundant. *Pleonasm* means using more words than necessary, *redundant* means using more words than necessary, and *tautological* means the needless repetition of an idea, statement or word.

349 Almost half a million times.

350 The Dutch, English and Swedes all claimed it, but the Swedes built the first permanent white settlement in Pennsylvania in 1638. In 1655 the Dutch took over from the Swedes and nine years after that the English took over from them.

351 Emmanuel Poiré called himself Caran d'Ache, the French spelling of the Russian for lead pencil.

352 Maria Cunitz, Caroline Herschel, Maria Mitchell and Agnes Clerke.

353 The king is dead: Arabic *al shāh-māt.*

354 Greasing the cartridges with "sacred" cattle fat. Part of the preparation for loading a gun involved biting the cartridge; it was against the religion of the Indian soldiers to kill a cow, let alone eat any part of one— even the grease.

355 In medieval England, under its full name Posse comitatus (from the Latin word *posse,* to have power, *comitatus,* a country). It meant an armed band with legal authority.

356 Only one extra dime is needed. The top one must just reach the two points of contact, P and P'.

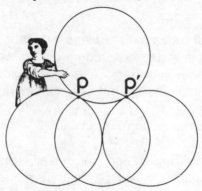

357 In the days of Elizabeth I, rails were made of wood for carts to move on, particularly on rough or soft ground.

358 Quintessence: it meant (according to the Pythagoreans) Ether, of which were made the heavenly bodies.

359 It is one of the worst poisons, and yet is the simplest compound: HCN, composed of three of the elements most necessary to life, hydrogen, carbon and nitrogen.

360 Benedict Arnold.

361 In talking about Ireland and England coming to a peaceful rapport, Sir Roche Boyle (1743−1807) said he hoped "the two sisters would embrace as one brother." It brought down the House (of Commons).

362 One solution is $1+1+2+2+3+3+4+4+5+5+6+6+7+7+8+8+9+9$

$$+\sqrt{(1+2+3+4+5+6+7+[8\times9])} = 100$$

363 Napoleon said, "Every French soldier carries a marshal's baton in his knapsack."

364 Agnes Sorel, c. 1420−1450.

365 Roger Bacon, in the middle of the thirteenth century. Franklin invented bifocals.

366 Elizabeth Blackwell, 1821−1910, sister-in-law of Lucy Stone.

367 Not sovereign. They derive from different words, sovereign from Latin *superanus,* chief; sovereignty from Latin *supremitas,* supreme power.

368 Lincoln was shot. Dundreary was in the play *Our American Cousin.*

369 Shoebill crane. Over five feet tall.

370 Ellen Terry, in boys' parts.

371 Drug-taker, prostitute, pickpocket. Writers often get them wrong.

372 They were all famous American artists who first became well known in England.

373 Madam Tussaud's Waxwork Museum. Holmes' address doesn't exist.

374 It is attributed to Dr. Spooner himself. On arriving at a house he said, "Please will you hush my brat, it's roaring with pain outside." He claimed he never said it, later.

375 A misreading of the spelling JHVH for Jahveh in Hebrew, which often ignores vowels.

376 Titian, who lived to 99.

377 Alpha Centauri; 4.3 light years or 25,000,000,000,000 miles.

378 He was highly adept in most sciences.

379 It is actually the view from above. All but the head stays on the ground.

380 Because some of them painted themselves black. Morris comes from Moorish, the early English name for all dark-skinned people. The word black referred to Gypsies as a rule, who are not dark.

381 Not until about A.D. 1200.

382 Luigi de Rossi's *Marriage d'Orphee et Euridice,* in the seventeenth century.

383 When two women claimed to be the mother of the same baby, he offered to cut the child in half and give half to each. Obviously the one who agreed was not the mother, so the other got the baby.

384 Two tiny metal balls hanging side by side on quartz filaments; they are used to weigh the Earth. The amount they attract one another is compared to their weight and by math the weight of the Earth is estimated. (Estimating the sun is done by analyzing optical effects and information.)

385 Urquhart's translation of three books of *Gargantua* by Rabelais, 1653–1693 (finished by P. A. Motteux). The Bible is great literature but is a mass of mistranslations.

386 They are "mob-proof," i.e., if the city were temporarily taken over in an insurrection it would be impossible to get at the vaults' contents for several days by any known means. Dynamite would bring the whole building down on the vaults.

387 A *meteor* is any small celestial object that becomes visible when it enters the Earth's atmosphere where friction may cause it to become incandescent. A *meteorite* is a meteor that has not burned up in the air and reaches the ground or sea. *Meteorology* is the science of weather, not meteors.

388 Britannia *rule* the waves, not *rules* the waves.

389 Two different ones: a fungus living symbiotically with an alga.

390 Not because it screeches, but because it was once thought to foretell death. A screech owl is also called a lich owl. (Anglo-saxon *lic,* body) cf. lichgate in a churchyard, the place where the coffins rest on the way to funerals or burials.

391 A red rose petal. Press it hard against some paper, and the resultant pink stain will have the same properties as litmus. In fact a rose blossom can be made a deep blue with ammonia.

392 Daniel Lambert, 1770–1809: 739 pounds, 102″ waist (average height).

393 Neither is a canine. The Tasmanian wolf is a marsupial, and the hyena is a member of the cat family.

394 So that they could ignore the commandment against killing, and yet not break the canonic rule against spilling blood.

395 Michigan touches Lakes Michigan, Superior, Huron and Erie.

396 What sinks to the bottom but is marked by a buoy attached to it by a rope for future recovery.

397 The eccentric Timothy Dexter of Newburyport, Mass., 1743–1802, who called himself Lord Timothy Dexter. There was a strike in Newcastle and so, for a change, they had no coals of their own.

398 The welding of popular melodies to medieval church harmonization techniques. It came rather late in France, oddly enough, perhaps because their *chansons* and nursery rhymes were so good they did not need the added church technique.

399 Silver, copper and gold, in that order.

400 *Cleavage* is splitting a gem, *brutage* is removing unwanted irregularities and projections.

401 Its height; they reach 400 feet.

402 Some third-person verbs: they run, he runs, etc.

403 It would seem that we can get there in a minimum of 4.3 years, but we must instead determine the maximum acceleration and deceleration a human body can stand to reach and return from a speed which has been approximated at 186,000 miles per second.

404 Maybe you can add to this list. (*Ctenoid* is the tricky one.)

```
IN.FA
  FACT
  ACT
    CTENOID
     TEN
      EN
       NO.ID
          IDEA
         DEA
         DEAR.SIR
           EAR.SIRLOIN
                LO.IN
                LOIN
                  INTIMATE
                       MA
                      MAT
                       AT
                        TEA
                        TEASE
                        EASE
                        AS
                          SEN
                          END
                          ENDING
                             DIN.GO
                             DINGO
                             IN.GOT
                               GOTHE
                                THEM
                                HE
                                HEM
                                 EM
```

405 Swan pan:

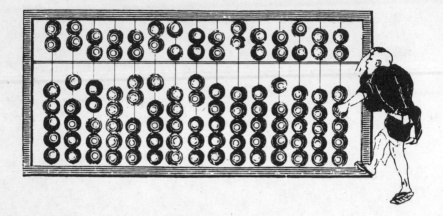

406 DOGMA I: I AM GOD

407 Southern, near the source; odd, since the word Nile is from *nila,* Sanskrit for indigo, blue. There the Nile *is* white.

408 Acceleration, not mere speed. Drag strips are usually short and straight.

409

L	yr	E
A	w	L
MacaronI		
B	a	A

410 Your sister. You have the same parents (children get half of their chromosomes from each parent, so you and your sister share the same chromosomes while you and your mother have only half of your chromosomes in common) and the same early environment.

411 Plants that close their petals at night, such as morning glories, four o'clocks, etc.

412 Sightseers.

413 1782, by J. M. and J. E. Montgolfier in France. It was 33 feet in diameter, made of linen, and smoke-filled because they mistakenly thought smoke was lighter than air (actually the hot air from the fire used to produce the smoke lifted it because hot air is lighter than cold air). First flight of a human was of F. P. de Rozier, 1783.

414 To an alchemist it meant sealed with the seal of Hermes (not the Greek god but the Egyptian Thoth).

415 Neither, because by a well-known theorem in Euclid the sum of the lengths of two tangents from a given point to the given circle plus the length of any tangent intersecting the two other tangents is constant.

416 They were all men. See any biographical dictionary.

417 Bested and worsted.

418 Ogam, an alphabet of twenty letters represented by notches (the vowels) and lines cut into the edges of memorial stones. Irish c. A.D. 600.

419 Ammonium, actually a radical NH_4 from which we derive ammonia and its compounds, some metallic.

420 Ampersand (&); the word means *and per se.*

421 Hemp, mentioned by Herodotus and the early Chinese, also mandragora; see Pliny.

422 Magnified potato starch granules.

423 He built a "high place" for the goddess Astarte, or "Astaroth."

424 Barbed wire. It made it possible to fence the open cattle range for farming and homesteading.

425 To state in his will that he leaves the land to them and "let one son divide the land and the other have first choice."

426 Not *The Game and Playe of Chess,* as is usually thought. The first English-language book was *The Recuyell of the Historyes of Troye,* printed in Bruges in 1474—1475. Then the first dated book in England was *The Dictes or Sayengis of the Philosophers,* in 1477. Prior to that a number of small pamphlets had been published.

427 "There are three_____s in the English language: to, too and two."

428 Yale's cheer "Brek-ek-ek-ek, Koax koax," is from Aristophane's play *The Frogs* (of course in the play it wasn't a cheer).

429 All three originated in China.

430 Plato.

431 Because it points to the Magnetic Pole instead of the geographical.

432 None to speak of before 1770, only bars, but by 1789 there were more than a hundred.

433 He was a boy wonder at mathematics, languages and versification, in the 1570's. He was called "The Admirable Crichton" by Urquhart (see qu. 385). J. M. Barrie took his name for a play written in 1902, but Barrie's play is not about the real Crichton, who was a Scottish gentleman and not an English butler.

434 The Gentleman's Hobbyhorse, c. 1817. (No pedals.)

435 Nine years, from 1660 to 1669.

436 Refers not to any mural but one painted on wet plaster; from Italian *fresco,* fresh.

437 *Punch,* designed by Richard Doyle.

438 The Dragon Lizards, living in the trees in the East Indies and southern Asia.

439 No one; it was an instrument of torture.

440 Galore, from *go leor,* enough.

441 Phonograph, movies, telephone transmitters (carbon particles).

442 Otto Von Guericke's electrostatic globe (1663) made of sulfur or glass which, when rotated and rubbed by hand, produced static electricity and magnetism. It had only experimental scientific value.

443 Jonas Hanway in 1786.

444 Three million square miles.

445 An auctioneer, who "upheld" objects for sale.

446 Me.

447 On the amount of labor that went into making a product. Contrary to general opinion rarity (e.g. of gold) was included as the amount of labor increased with the difficulty of finding a particular item.

448 Paris. Not New York; Manhattan is fairly large.

449 The little star on Norman pennies, from Anglo-Saxon *steorra,* star.

450 Saint Veronica lent hers to Christ to wipe his brow while carrying the cross.

451 Calves. Veterinarian is from *vitulis,* which means calf in Latin.

452 He was a reformed criminal. Later in life he relapsed in an attempt to gain attention and reemployment. He organized a big heist and informed on his coworkers, pretending skillful detective powers. He then organized his own agency but it flopped, and he died in obscurity.

453 The Villanelle: ABA, ABA, ABA, ABA, ABA, ABAA (only two rhymes).

454 François Villon, pseudonym of the famous poet. No one is sure of his real name. (De Montcorbier? Des Loges?)

455 They were called Nuremberg Eggs, because of their shape. The date was about 1500. They were the size of an alarm clock and hung on the belt.

456 The finger acts as a jig, or holder to present what is to be worked on, or bowed, by the right hand.

457 The African has one, the Asiatic has two.

458 (1) Yes. Try it and see. (2) One side still cannot be greater than the sum of the other two. Any three points make a triangle, but any three straight lines do not necessarily do so.

459 An early form of whist called *La Triomphe*.

460 "Not the work of an hour but the knowledge of a lifetime."

461 They are Samelats, living in Sabine.

462 William Kembler at Auburn, New York in 1890.

463 Queen Elizabeth I.

464 Fold diagonal, then short fold at right angles to diagonal to corner, which will give 3″.

Proof: ΔADB is similar to ΔABC, since angle BAD is common to both and both contain right angles. Therefore $\dfrac{AB}{AC} = \dfrac{BD}{BC}$. The value of AC may be determined by the Pythagorean theorem. Substituting all known values:

$$\frac{\frac{15}{4} \times 5}{5^2 + \left(\frac{15}{4}\right)^2} = BD$$

$$\frac{75}{4} \times \frac{4}{25} = BD$$

$$3 = BD$$

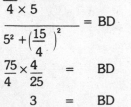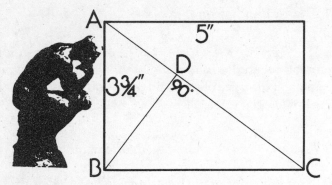

465 They used to be good.

466 Glass.

467 Lavinia Fontana, Italy, 1552–1614.

468 First hold the two brushes with arms crossed, right hand at A, left at B. Then move A to H, halfway down, then bring left hand down from B crossing over red line at X and continue to bottom. Then continue down with right hand crossing over blue line to bottom. (Don't sign it.)

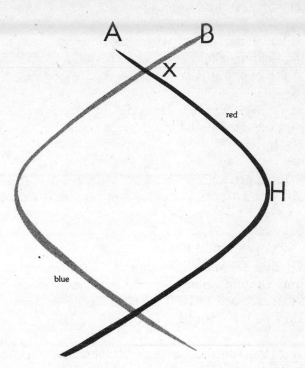

469 The all-time hit *The Beggar's Opera,* written by John Gay and produced by John Rich in London in 1728.

470 Ben Jonson, 1617.

471 There are infinity points in a finite area, also parallel straight lines in that area, but infinitely *more* unspecified curved lines of variable shape and length. Why, I don't know.

472 A gnomon.

473 The giant crab.

474 The angles of a crystal.

475 1865. It broke, but when the first non-breaking one was laid near it in 1886, they mended the 1865 cable, which could thus finally be termed successful.

476 In 1839 Charles Goodyear dropped some unvulcanized, semi-liquid rubber mixed with sulfur onto a hot stove.

477 It has been called Gresham's Law, by Macleod, but was much earlier stated by Oresme and Copernicus.

478 Chile.

479 UT queant laxis, REsonare fibris, MIra gestorum, FAmuli tuorum, SOLve polluti, LAbia reatum. UT has been changed to DO; the complete scale from C up is; Do Re Mi Fa So(l) La Ti Do.

480 Not increasing the time of cooking, but increasing the temperature and thereby *lessening* the time.

481 Japan is a lot longer, 2,100 miles.

482 Henry Ossawa Tanner, exhibited and known mainly in France.

483 "Night and Day" by Cole Porter. The melodic line running through Berlioz's *Harold in Italy* is neither sung nor is it uninterrupted. The Wagner *lieder* are far shorter—they merely repeat. William Ames' "Augurs" is not all sung by one person in spite of its terrific sense of coherence.

484 He was the original of Shakespeare's Yorick. ("I knew him, Horatio.")

485 Thebes in Greece and in Egypt.

486 The three-body problem, i.e., determining the motions of three bodies moving under the influence of their mutual gravitational masses only.

487 Strictly speaking in terms of the five, we must ignore such ones as the sense of acceleration or the angle at which the head is tilted (the latter is felt by the semicircular canals in the ear). There are, however, two senses of heat, one set of nerves for hot and one for cold. If the latter is over-stimulated we feel heat, as when we say burning but icy. This may be partly due to the heat sensors being also affected by extreme cold. Is pain a sense? Is tickling? Who can say?

488 From a classic word meaning a wild beast. Treacle was supposed to be an antidote against the possible venom. Today treacle is the British word for molasses.

489 For being the first to suggest the use of iron for shipbuilding. About 1810.

490 A trivet—a cooking support—has three legs, and is thus always firm.

491 *A poet who'd finished a line with "betimes"*
Felt okay as he knew there were simply dozens of
*   rhymes,*

But he unfortunately ended the next one with "dwarf,"
And that meant he'd have to have it all happening on
   a wharf.
Or to be exacter,
He'd have to refer to Richard the actor.

492 The type letters were not separate and thus "movable" but were cut by hand on one block of wood for each page.

493 An electrical discharge (visible) from ship masts upward to the sky. Lightning appears to travel a reverse route, but modern scientists are uncertain as to which way it starts as it is evidently an alternating current.

494 It comes from Latin *cisorium,* a cutting instrument, from which Middle English *cisors.* The *s* was added by phony Latin scholars a little later.

495 We imagine a vertical bisector which by Pythagoras measures four. By a well-known Euclidean lemma the diameter of a circle that fits into a right triangle equals the sum of the adjacent sides minus the hypotenuse. In this case, the answer is two. Q.E.D.

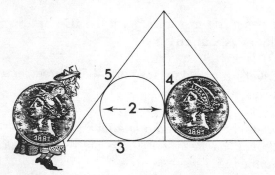

496 Precisely the same as the flag of the East India Company, with the Union Jack in the corner and horizontal stripes.

497 The Taj Mahal in Agra, India. Unfairly, because some people (myself included) disagree.

498 No water; it meant a massage and still does, in India.

499 The Slavs.

500 Gloves. The others are perhaps wrap-arounds, but we can't be sure.

501 Mercaptan—the smelliest-known chemical—can be detected by the presence of one 400 millionth of a milligram of it. (It is put in the bottom of tanks of gas to alert the cook that it has nearly run out.)

502 You.

503 Not a ruby as is usually thought, but a spinel of a ruby red color.

504 Hershel invented the blueprint copying process.

505 Sir Roland Hill, who had been a boy-wonder mathematician, introduced postage stamps bearing the same charge regardless of distance (within Great Britain) in 1840. He believed that processing mail was the main expense and transportation the least, and that the new system would increase the use of mail.

506 K2, Godwin Austen, 22,250 feet. Also in the Himalayas.

507 They suggest spelling changes, but actually they respectively were the old ways of writing capital F and Th.

508 When laid one on the other they spell W H A T A R E T H E Y D O I N G. (Trace the second on tracing paper and put it on the first one and see.)

509 M and N, eight times each.

510 The Moon creates tides which in turn led to life forms accommodating themselves to air breathing and the lack of water environment.

511 Thomas "Old" Parr, died aged 152: 1483–1635. There is said to be a woman 200 years old or more in Europe now, but it is not verifiable, as there are no reliable records of her birth.

512 It comes from another counting song, "I give you one-oh, *Green grow* the rushes-oh." It was once popular in the United States. The Mexicans heard U.S. soldiers singing it and referred to the singers as *gringos*.

513 Peter the Wild Boy, found wandering in the woods near Hanover, brought to England and stayed there in the eighteenth century. He couldn't speak when found, but later learned to, and was not mentally retarded.

514 Tin. There is sometimes no lead in it.

515 Dr. Grey of the British Museum began collecting

stamps in 1841. His became one of the finest collections in the world.

516 Not Jeanne d'Arc, but Jeanetton Darc; no apostrophe, and no such place as Arc.

517 Calcium phosphate.

518 Joseph N. de Niepce: a still life, c. 1810. He was aided by Daguerre. No portraits at first; they needed too long a sitting.

519 The first true piano, in the eighteenth century.

520 The pineapple is neither a pine nor an apple.

521 The bowl was in the center of the tube:

522 Six, three Louis II's and three Louis III's.

523 For very quick aiming. If we point at an object the angle between the forefinger and the gripping fingers, thumb and palm is the same as the angle under question. This was of course before putting sights on pistols.

524 An expert on shorthand writing.

525 Between Spain and the German Empire, April 1544.

526 Into the slightly inaccurately estimated distance between Paris and the North Pole.

527 Serving the state with your children.

528 To play the harp.

529 1860, England, Tom Sayers and the American J. C. Heenana; it ended in a draw.

530 Four: Queen Regnant, ruler in her own right; Queen Consort, the wife of a reigning king; Queen Dowager, widow of a former king; Queen Mother, mother of a present king.

531 "If you want a suitle, something episcutle, something in a three-button fancy drape: Hi, ho, lack-a-day, the World Clothing Exchange!" c. 1924, New York.

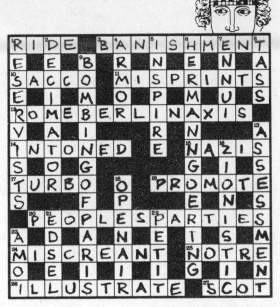

The crossword solution grid reads:

R	I	D	E		B	A	N	I	S	H	M	E	N	T
E		E	B		R		N		E		N			A
S	A	C	C	O		M	I	S	P	R	I	N	T	S
E		I	M		O		P		M		U			S
R	O	M	E	B	E	R	L	I	N	A	X	I	S	
V		A	I			R		N						A
I	N	T	O	N	E	D		E		N	A	Z	I	S
S		O	G						G		I			S
T	U	R	B	O		O		P	R	O	M	O	T	E
S			F		P			E		N		S		S
	P	E	O	P	L	E	S	P	A	R	T	I	E	S
A		D		A	N		E		T		S		M	
M	I	S	C	R	E	A	N	T		N	O	T	R	E
O		E		I			I			G		I		N
I	L	L	U	S	T	R	A	T	E			S	C	O	T

533 In no way. She may have had "seven demons cast out of her" but who didn't in those days? She was a friend of Christ and went with him on his last journey to Jerusalem, saw the crucifixion and spoke to the risen Christ after death. She is often confused with the unnamed "fallen woman" at Simon's house, who anointed Christ's feet. Also confused with Mary of Bethany, sister of Lazarus.

534 Meteors.

535 A lemma in Euclid says that the locus of points from which two tangents are drawn to any two circles is a straight line, provided that the distance from the points to the tangents remain equal. The locus is at right angles to the line joining the centers of the circles. (The elastic stretches with the same resistance at all parts.)

536 The United States. There are fifty-two sets of laws: one each for the fifty states and Washington, D.C., and the Federal Code.

537

538 You are absolutely right!